D0396056

# SMART WOMEN KEEP IT SIMPLE

# SMART WOMEN KEEP IT SIMPLE

## ANNIE CHAPMAN
WITH
## MAUREEN RANK

BETHANY HOUSE PUBLISHERS
Minneapolis, Minnesota 55438

Published by Bethany House Publishers
A Ministry of Bethany Fellowship, Inc.
6820 Auto Club Road, Minneapolis, Minnesota 55438

Printed in the United States of America

Library of Congress Cataloging-in-Publication Data

Chapman, Annie.
    Smart women keep it simple / Annie Chapman with Maureen Rank.
        p.   cm.
    Includes bibliographical references.

    1. Women—Religious life.   2. Chapman, Annie.   3. Rank, Maureen.
I. Rank, Maureen.   II. Title.
BV4527.C47   1992
248.8'43—dc20                                              91-39550
ISBN 1–55661–236–2                                        CIP

I dedicate this book to the three men in my life who have taught me that being a woman is a tremendous honor:

To my dad, Ney Williamson, who showed me what the heavenly Father is like.

To Steve, my husband, who makes me want to be what he thinks I already am.

To Nathan, my son, who gives me hope for the future and a glorious benediction to the past.

## Books by Annie Chapman (with Maureen Rank)

Gifts Your Kids Can't Break
Married Lovers, Married Friends
Smart Women Keep It Simple

## Books by Maureen Rank

Dealing With the Dad of Your Past
Free to Grieve

ANNIE CHAPMAN has been ministering to families with her husband Steve through their music and speaking for many years. They have several albums and books in national distribution, their music and message on the family have been featured in numerous magazines, and they perform nationwide in concerts every year. The Chapmans make their home in Nashville.

MAUREEN RANK is a graduate from Iowa State University and spent six years on the Navigators staff ministering to college students. She is the author of eight books, including *Married Lovers, Married Friends, Dealing With the Dad of Your Past*, and *Free to Grieve*. She and her husband live in Knoxville, Iowa, and have two children.

# Contents

# 1

# Simply
# Devoted

# When the Plates Won't All Stay Spinning

Because their parents are musicians, our children Heidi and Nathan have grown up "on the
road." Some experiences we've savored, such as
seeing exciting places or meeting celebrities.
Other experiences have proved to be downright
unsavory.

Years ago we traveled in a van. When Nathan
became toilet-trainable, we outfitted the van with
a little plastic potty chair. It was an impressive
model: when water hit the bottom of the bowl,
the chair began to tinkle a tune—either "Row,
Row, Row Your Boat" or "Raindrops Keep Falling
on My Head"; I can't remember which.

We soon learned, however, that once the chair
had served its purpose, we should rid ourselves
of the contents as quickly as possible or suffer
probable asphyxiation from the foul fumes.

So one Tuesday in May, when we pulled up
to a church where we'd be singing, I hopped out

of the van and headed for the restroom, carefully balancing the loaded potty chair. When I opened the door to the foyer, however, the bowl slid from the chair, cascading its contents right toward the deep-plush carpet.

By an act of heaven's mercy, there happened to be a large piece of plastic covering that part of the carpet. I yelled to a teenage boy standing inside the door to help me grab the plastic. With each of us holding two corners, we gingerly carried it down the hall to the men's room and emptied its contents without spilling a drop. (I chose the men's room as an act of kindness. I felt the teenager had been through quite enough without subjecting him to the added humiliation of being seen going into a ladies' restroom!)

We later learned that the plastic was even more of a godsend than we first thought. The carpet was new, and the pastor valued it so highly he wouldn't even allow coffee in the foyer. Imagine how warmly he'd have welcomed us if we'd emptied our porta-potty on the carpet!

In case you think I'm one of those annoying parents who loves to tell and retell her toilet-training stories, let me explain why I'm passing on one of our most embarrassing moments.

My life, like yours, is full of a thousand demands. Sometimes I feel yanked this way and that . . . totally off-balance. When I do, I think of that piece of plastic being carried so cautiously down the hall, and I tell myself, "Annie, you'd better keep life in balance, or you're going to wind up with a real mess on your hands!"

When I become unbalanced and wonder how

it happened, the Bible offers this explanation: "A doubleminded man [or woman]," James 1:8 says, "[is] unstable in all he does."

Some women say yes to the Lord and no to the world. Others say yes to the world, but no to the Lord. But the doubleminded woman says yes to everything! Consequently, she's continually off-balance, like a drunken high-wire artist, lurching dangerously along the wire, leaning first to this side, then to that. She's a cataclysmic fall just waiting to happen.

Nobody wants to be doubleminded. But how do we know when to say yes, and when no is the better answer? Is the key to balance making snappier do-lists, or prioritizing more efficiently, or ceasing to be so co-dependent?

I don't think so. The answer is easier than any of these things, and also much harder. Paul says, "I am afraid that just as Eve was deceived by the serpent's cunning, your minds may somehow be led astray from the simplicity and purity of devotion to Christ" (2 Corinthians 11:3, NASB).

Simple, pure devotion to Christ—that's the prescription for a life in balance. The balanced woman is not out to please some of the people all the time, or all of the people some of the time. She's not committed to please anyone at all . . . except Christ. Her strategy for living is to be simply, purely, passionately devoted to the Lord.

## Growing in Devotion

I can't decide where I want to go until I know where I am. That's why the first step toward devotion must be *evaluation*. Knowing the strengths and weaknesses in my marriage, my mothering, and my mission helps me see where devotion to Christ thrives already, and where it needs to grow.

Next, I need to *eliminate* attitudes that keep me from devotion. The five I see as most destructive are condemnation, covetousness, cursing, comparisons, and competition.

Lastly, *establishing* life patterns of acceptance, endurance, and vision will keep me devoted when the going gets tough.

When I die, I'd like these words carved on my tombstone: "Here lies Annie Chapman; she was simply devoted to Christ." Evaluating, eliminating, and establishing all sound like wonderful ideas! But I'll be honest. At this moment in my life, I'm feeling more demented than devoted. If smart women keep it simple, there are times when I feel as dumb as a stump!

Last Tuesday, for example, the alarm sounded and I groaned. It couldn't be 6:00 A.M. already, but it was. A new day dawning, and I was still yawning. And something wasn't right about this day . . . something hung over me, causing unnamed dread.

Yikes! This was the day I promised I'd weigh myself. The homemade sugar cookies and that big bag of potato chips had been glorious, but the time had come to confront the scales and assess the damage.

I climbed on, savagely sucking in my stomach, as if this would somehow lighten the load. It was as bad as I feared. I was four pounds from where

I wanted to be, which was three pounds from what I should be. So, ahead lay another day of cruel deprivation. Guilty and disgruntled, I trudged into the morning.

There are days, like that Tuesday, when I'm not sure how I'm going to get through. Sometimes I panic at the thought of just trying to get everything done, not to mention giving enough emphasis to the things that matter most. Devotion to Christ seems like a pipe dream.

If you are old enough, you'll remember the Ed Sullivan Show. My most vivid Sullivan memory centers on a juggler who started twirling a china plate, then placed it high in the air on top of a pole. He'd get one plate balanced and turning, and then he'd start another. Before long the stage was filled with plates twirling atop long slender poles. The juggler would then frantically run back and forth keeping each plate in motion so it wouldn't wobble and crash to the floor.

What a picture of my life! The "plates" I'm trying to keep aloft are all precious to me. They begin with my relationships with those I value most: God and my husband.

Most difficult to keep in the air are the stable relationships with my children. At this moment, I am parent to a teenage son and a pre-teen daughter, and there is no season of life more raw than adolescence. It's full of skin eruptions, growing pains, awkward limbs that stick out every which way, hurt feelings, and broken hearts. The only thing worse than going through adolescence is watching someone you love traverse it.

Being there for an adolescent is like watching

someone go through labor and delivery. My friend's husband wound up in prison while she was to deliver their baby, so as a baby gift, I offered to pay for childbirth classes and serve as her coach in the delivery room.

When the big day finally came, we did our pant-pant-blow routine while she contracted. I tried to be patient, but I'll confess, after an hour of watching her push and strain, I was exhausted. Every time she'd bear down, so would I. Finally I wanted to scream, "All right, you've had your chance! I've done this twice before, so get off that table and let me have a turn at it!"

I often hold those same feelings about my children's teen traumas. I want to say, "Okay, son, I've done it before and I can do it again. Get out of my way, and let me handle it!" Of course this works no better than trying to take over another woman's delivery. Keeping the "plate" of each of my children spinning evenly takes more energy and grace every year.

In the midst of one of my parenting panic attacks, Steve came up with the lyrics to a song he titled "Ode to a Mom":

> Survivor's the name given to those
> Who've lived through wars and disasters.
> And it is the name I'd gladly wear—
> In fact, it's the name I'm after.
> For today there've been wars 'tween me and
>     my children
> As they've turned my clean house into rubble.
> The wise man must have been thinking of
>     moms
> When he said, "Our days are few and full of

nothin' but trouble."

But if I'm alive when this day is done,
I will be numbered among the ones
Who've lived through the wars
And passed through the fires.
Someday they might call me blessed,
But today I'll settle for *survivor.*

There is a name for those who would say
I ought to think higher than I'm thinking
    today,
And go for a name like "hero with honors."
I know they mean well . . . we call them
    fathers.

But if I'm alive when this day is done,
I will be numbered among the ones
Who've lived through the wars
And passed through the fires.
Someday they might call me blessed,
But today I'll settle for *survivor.*[1]

Just surviving while I keep my family "plates"
spinning isn't my only obligation. Besides household responsibilities, I've created professional demands outside my home that I'm obligated to fill.
I have book projects I'm working on, sometimes
several at once. Steve and I travel full-time in a
singing ministry. We also have recording projects,
song-writing sessions, concert preparations,
speaking engagements, and business details to
deal with.

---

[1]Words and music by Steve Chapman, Times and Seasons Music BMI,
used by permission.

On the side, I'm balancing "plates" of the friends to whom I'm committed. As they struggle with marital problems, parenting disappointments, and life's losses, I want to support them. I also feel a responsibility to the work of the church, while civic obligations press in. This week, for example, the Band Boosters are after me for bake-sale donations. "You do have a son in the marching band, don't you?" the voice on the telephone reminds me in a tone thick with accusation.

Perhaps even more emotionally charged for me at this moment in life is the "plate" that represents the needs of my parents, who are both in poor health. Now my brothers and sisters and I are very concerned for the well-being for those who were always there to care for us, and it makes us sad to see the tables turning.

There has to be a refuge, a place of peace and relief from this juggling act. My "plates" that need twirling are all precious to me. I can't afford to let even one of them drop. Because they're all essential, I must find a way to juggle them well.

Jesus Christ is the refuge I seek, the One who helps me keep life balanced and moving, because I simply can't do it by myself. Knowing He loves me brings back simplicity to my day.

As I mature, life seems increasingly out of control. When Heidi and Nathan were small, life held daily challenges, but I didn't have as many plates in the air as I do now. The days seemed full, but manageable. Sometimes I look back on the simplicity of those days nostalgically. But I've found I can still feel that quiet sense of simplicity in the midst of chaos if I try to only devote myself to pleasing Christ.

He's the One who helps me know if I have too many or too few plates in the air. Then He commits all His resources to helping keep those plates aloft that He wants me to spin. On the days when life squeezes the breath out of me, I can find simplicity as He helps me face one moment at a time.

Devotion to Christ is feeling that extra shoulder next to mine as I try to carry a load that's much too heavy for me. It's having an extra pair of hands to help me when responsibilities seem overwhelming. Even in the throes of difficulty, life can still be simple if I remain devoted to Christ, and allow Him to devote himself to me at the moment when I most need His loving touch.

This kind of devotion is what we'll explore together as we begin by evaluating. First, there's the marriage . . .

# 2

# Evaluating
# Your Marriage

# Partnership, Passion, and Priorities

The date: November 22, 1963.

The place: Second-floor hallway of Central Junior High School.

Just as the tardy bell rang, an event happened that would shake my personal world forever (and it wasn't the assassination of President Kennedy): Steve Chapman said hello to me.

Giddy teenage girl that I was, I hoped it meant he'd finally been captivated by my big green eyes, and soon intended to follow his "hello" with a marriage proposal.

No such luck. Steve's real interest at that point had much more to do with my father's farmland, on which he hoped to do some serious hunting. City-slickers like Steve (from Point Pleasant, West Virginia, population 8,000), often found themselves inexplicably drawn to girls like me (from a farm nine miles from anything even remotely urban), especially if they loved to shoot wild game and had no hunting grounds of their own.

I boasted not only access to a 120 acres, but an older brother who the year before had taken down an eleven-point buck and might be persuaded to take his sister's beau along to the very deer stand where the kill took place.

Not wanting to thwart true love, my brother Clarence did agree to take Steve hunting, although he showed no great enthusiasm when Steve pulled him out of bed three hours before daylight the morning they were scheduled to go. While the guys were out committing their manly acts of barbarism toward helpless animals, Mom and I made a hearty hunter's lunch, and waited for their noon arrival. I was, needless to say, a little breathless at the thought of sharing fried chicken and biscuits with the handsome Steve Chapman, and cooked with an ardor only an adolescent female in love can muster.

But our romantic encounter over the apple pie was not to be. Twelve-thirty passed, and no Steve. One o'clock came and went; still no sign of Steve. Finally about 1:30, I spotted him coming down off the hill, but instead of heading for the house, he went straight to his car and sped away. At that moment I understood the agony of defeat, and my mother was so disgusted she vowed she'd "never cook that boy another meal!"

We later learned that in the frigid temperatures of the early morning, Steve's watch had frozen. By the time he discovered it had stopped working, he was late getting the car back to his father, who needed it for work. Naturally, I forgave him, and apparently my mother did, too, because she's reneged on her vow about never cooking for him too many times to count.

In the high school years ahead, our friendship continued to grow. After graduation we went our separate ways—Steve to college and then into the military, while I enrolled in Moody Bible Institute.

When we reconnected, much had changed. After his discharge from the Navy, Steve had become a bona fide hippie and had gotten into the music business in Nashville. In contrast, I had adopted the look of a plain-faced, hair-in-a-bun spinster missionary, and had joined a ministry to inner-city children in Philadelphia. We met again while we were visiting our parents in West Virginia. Although physically we looked about as compatible as Cher and Richard Nixon, we found as we talked that our interests and basic life values were still very much in sync. It didn't take long for the friendship we'd begun all those years before to ignite into a fire. In 1974, Steve finally asked, "Annie, wilt thou?" I wilted, and I haven't revived yet.

I'm very grateful for the way God designed Steve to be partner, lover, and friend to me. In *Married Lovers, Married Friends* we wrote about the ways we grow together as a couple. But other issues about marriage are important for women who want to keep their lives simple—issues of partnership, passion, and priorities.

## Growing as Partners

The Christian church has spent a great deal of time fussing over the issue of submission. For a while, all we heard at women's retreats was why we ought to submit; now we're hearing why we shouldn't. Personally, I consider all this fracas unnecessarily blown out of proportion.

When I think of my life with Steve, the best description that comes to mind is found in Philippians 4:3, when Paul calls his friend a "loyal yokefellow." When I read that, a light bulb turned on in my mind. Steve and I are yokefellows to each other. We're like two strong oxen yoked together to pull a load for Christ. Together we can manage more than twice what either could pull separately. On the wagon, we can carry our children, our families, and others the Lord has given us to minister to. It doesn't matter which ox is stronger at a particular time; it matters only that the load arrives safely at its destination.

Yoked up with Steve, I need to pull my half, or the wagon won't remain steady. So it is in our marriage. I trust his leadership, but unless I add thoughtful input to the decisions, question when I don't agree, and heartily support the decision once it's made, I'm not pulling half the load. I'm a freeloader, not a yokefellow.

Our team effort is well illustrated when we go to purchase a car. Steve believes that the sticker price is what the salesman absolutely has to have just to break even. I, on the other hand, view it as the "stick-it-to-'em" price. Steve tempers my horse trader's "leave-'em-bleeding" spirit of negotiation with his easy-going, "would you like my first-born also?" spirit.

Besides sharing the work, being a yokefellow means sharing the blame. Not all the decisions

Steve and I have made together have been good ones.

A friend who does financial planning came upon a great opportunity he knew we shouldn't pass up—a great tax break, he said, and a wonderful chance to invest God's money wisely!

We aren't financial wizards, but we decided together to trust the advice of our friend, the expert. We prayed about the decision together, but a clear answer never came. Finally we concluded that God must be saying, "Just use your own judgment."

We did, and have we regretted it! A few weeks after finalizing the deal, Congress changed all the tax laws, and we were left with a financial albatross around our necks.

But at least when we get letters concerning the "perfectly safe investment" that has eaten our lunch financially for the last several years, neither of us can blame the other. We walked together as equals into this silly agreement, so we suffer equitably.

## Working Out the Push and Pull

Because we share the yoke, it's wrong to expect Steve to drag me along, but it's equally wrong for me to try to pull the wagon all by myself. I need to let him pull his weight, too.

Sometimes women do too much. Maybe we're not sure our husbands are going to lead, or the way they lead doesn't suit us. But when we carry the share that's rightfully theirs, they weaken, and wind up carrying less and less. We'll eventually find ourselves feeling trapped and victimized by their helplessness.

James Walker, a pastor and counselor, says,

> When a man's position is challenged or thwarted, he will retreat, giving less to the marriage. He may stop bringing his personality, his energy, and his creativity home. A woman's natural tendency then is to assume the space that has been vacated by her husband. She becomes more than she should in order to make up for his emotional absence and to restore the home to working order.
>
> She initiates conversation because "he won't talk." She takes over all the bill-paying because "they'll turn out the lights." She opens the Bible and reads to the children, and she prays with them because "my kids won't get anything spiritual from their father." What results is a functioning family unit, but one that's in the process of dying.

Walker tells the story of Jane, who decided she'd pulled the wagon long enough for her "party boy" husband, Eric. One of the few places he'd agree to help in the home was in taking out the garbage. However, when the task actually needed doing, he was always too busy, or waiting for the next commercial, or had his hands full, or something. Jane became tired of nagging and took the garbage out herself. The same thing happened with bill-paying. Eric told her to throw the bills on his desk and he'd take care of them, but they were never paid until panic forced her to do it herself.

Finally, she decided to stop mothering her

husband. The next time the garbage needed to go out, she asked only once. After that, she started filling paper sacks beside the overflowing garbage can. The rest of the family made a fuss, but it took her husband five days of walking past the pile of refuse to notice it.

"I asked you to take that out the other day," Jane replied calmly. "I knew you'd get to it whenever you were able." She quietly communicated confidence in her husband, but also a line she would not cross.

Later, Jane took a similar action about the payment of their bills. Instead of bailing Eric out, she honored his commitment that he'd pay them. He didn't, of course, but after bill collectors began hounding him, he realized his wife was no longer going to mother him.

He said later, "I knew that all my life I just tried to get by. I didn't think of myself as lazy, but I suppose I was. I know I wasn't God's prize-husband. Jane deserved better. But that day it hit me. *Things weren't going to get any better if I didn't change.*"

What Jane had been trying to accomplish for twelve years, the bill collectors and garbage odors took care of in three months!

"In marriage," Walker says, "three things can change: the wife, her mate, and their relationship. A woman can decide to change at least two of those three. Any movement in her own life will change their relationship. If she changes, he must make adjustments in response to her."[1]

---

[1]James Walker, *Husbands Who Won't Lead and Wives Who Won't Follow*, (Minneapolis: Bethany House Publishers, 1989), p. 101.

Jane chose to set a limit in a place I couldn't have. Fears of a bad credit rating would have pushed me to give in and pay those bills. This woman apparently knew she could tolerate this pressure without folding. If you need to set limits on the loads you carry, think carefully about where you'll say, "This is the job you've agreed to do and I won't take it on anymore." Be sure you're really willing to let go and leave the consequences with God and your husband, or you'll just be playing a mind game, and not really attempting to minister to your husband's needs. God doesn't bless manipulation, but He will bless courage that springs from love.

## Growing in Passion

How thankful I am that when God thought of marriage, He decided to add sex to the mix! It's a beautiful bonding element that only He, in His creativity and love, could have designed.

But sex wasn't created simply for pleasure. God also gave it as a way that women can minister to their husbands—a way no one else on earth is able to. In Proverbs 5:18, 19, Solomon counsels his son, "Rejoice in the wife of your youth. . . . Be exhilarated always with her love."

Although this instruction is God's command to men, I take it as a challenge to me as well. As the years go on, I want to continue to offer a pleasant appearance and a tender embrace so that rejoicing in the wife of his youth isn't a chore for my husband.

One way I can do this is to not let myself get

frumpy. Even though Steve has seen me at my very worst, and loves me anyway, I want that "worst" to be the exception, rather than the rule. When we go out together, I want the lady on his arm to be one that brings him pride. And when we're home alone, I want him to know he's important enough that I'll look good just for him.

A friend who recently attended a Christian family conference told me how men there expressed their opinions on this subject. In sort of a newlywed-game format, the speaker asked the men to list what was most important to them in a mate, and the women to do the same. When the men shared their answers, most of the women were astounded to find that "physical attractiveness" rated #2 or #3 on nearly every man's list.

The male of our species is a visual creature, and he takes pleasure from visual stimuli. So, I'm determined that Mr. Chapman is going to have something pretty to look at when he looks at me. He's not going to get some starlet, of course, considering what I have to work with, but I'm doing what I can to insure that what he gets smells good, looks trim, and dresses attractively.

That scripture in Proverbs also challenges me to provide a tender embrace, but it doesn't say I always have to feel like it. A woman's sexual satisfaction is important, of course. But sometimes there can be great satisfaction in knowing I've been able to meet my husband's needs, even though I wasn't feeling the same intensity of need myself. We don't always have to be swept away by great waves of passion in order to make love.

Loving at its best means giving what I have for the good of another.

Because of his commitment to faithfulness, my beloved has limited himself to find satisfaction for his desires in my arms alone. I can honor his commitment by providing that satisfaction aggressively and sweetly, even if I'm not exactly "in the mood." Loving and serving each other keeps our intimate moments together special.

## Growing in Each Other's Priorities

Steve and I were asked to sing on a television show for a now well-known, but then local preacher. As this minister spoke into the camera about how wonderful his marriage was, I glanced over at his wife, who was sitting just out of camera range. On her face was a look of utter disgust and bitter anguish.

I concluded that either the preacher was a bold-faced liar, or his eyes were blinded to the hurt his wife was feeling. In either case, the one who tried to minister to others had missed his most important ministry.

But we've seen Christian women make the same mistake.

Counselor James Walker agrees:

> I am sad to say that I have seen spiritually mature and extremely gifted women who have had magnificent ministries to others, but mates whom they only refer to in an embarrassed and apologetic manner. I've talked with their husbands, who silently remain in the background and have beat a hasty and intim-

idated retreat from the spiritual leadership of their home and even their own lives. As a group, these "spiritual drones" are among the angriest men I know.[2]

Walker goes on to remind women that if they truly mean to serve Christ, they should ask themselves, "I may be committed to this marriage—but am I equally dedicated to the man who is in the marriage with me?" If we have that kind of dedication, we'll ask ourselves, "What are my husband's needs, and how can God use me to supply them?"[3]

One of the most essential ways we supply each other's needs is by giving the gift of time. What we do with our time indicates whom and what we really love. Yet often we overlook the importance of time alone with each other. Spending valuable time together won't happen without a plan. Life closes in on us and will take up every free second unless we work at getting alone with the one we love most.

Even though Steve and I travel together, we find we still have to get away for what I call "soul" time. Traveling means sharing a motel room with two kids, and outside the motel we are continually surrounded by other people. We can communicate the day to day business of life, but deep sharing simply doesn't happen between us when we're with others. That's why when we come home we often go out to lunch, just the two of us. Or we check into a nearby inexpensive motel

[2]Ibid., p. 165.
[3]Op. cit.

for the afternoon while the kids are in school—partly for the joy of unhurried physical intimacy, but also to allow us to be together without the interrupters that keep us from focusing on each other, such as the telephone, the laundry, or the lawnmower, to name a few.

I'm also learning to get needed time with Steve by saying yes when he asks, "Do you want to ride along to the hardware store?" or "Would you like to go out in the boat with me this afternoon?"

Because I'm a workaholic, my instinctive response to requests like these is always negative. I never feel I have time for nonessentials; I'm always weighed down by work beckoning me.

People sometimes say to me, "Don't worry about the dirty dishes, Annie. They'll still be there when you get back." They somehow think this comment frees me to enjoy myself. Now, if a fairy godmother were to fly in and wash those dishes while I was out, *that* would comfort me, but the thought of walking back into the house to a stack of dirty dishes does not comfort me.

I have finally decided, however, that work—like death and taxes—is one of life's certainties. If I choose not to play until the work is all done, I'll never play this side of heaven. Steve's invitations give me that chance to play, and needed time with him, as well.

On a larger scale, you may need to think more aggressively about your responsibilities. If you and your husband can't seem to get relaxed time together, maybe you need to rid yourself of some extra duties. For the sake of your companionship, you may need to hire help with the cleaning, for example, or work harder at getting the children to share the load of household tasks. Your husband may also need to resign from some committee or expendable responsibility. Even cutting back on daily phone calls to friends may help free up some time.

A few years ago I left the board of a Christian counseling service for this very reason. Although they represented a cause we supported wholeheartedly, their meeting fell on the only weekend of the month that I had off to be home with the family. The cause was worthy, but the time commitment was too much. Whatever it takes to make space for the two of you, do it.

One woman told me, "When I'd get under stress with the kids, my husband would often suggest that we get away for a day. I'd invariably protest, We can't afford to! Then he'd shake his head firmly in disagreement: 'We can't afford not to!' "

Lastly, make a priority of your _time alone_. It's vital that you and your husband be alone together; it's equally vital that you each be alone at times. Steve's creativity and sanity depend on his time by himself. When he suggests a game of golf, I send him off with a smile and a wish for a great game, not a whining, "You're leaving me alone with the kids _again_?" He returns the favor when I need time for myself, whether it's planning a women's retreat, finishing a chapter for a book, or just rest and quiet.

Marriage is a lifetime proposition. It requires

a lifetime of fine-tuning to keep two yokefellows pulling together, loving, serving, and enjoying each other.

# 3

# Evaluating
# Your Mothering

# Mothering Without Smothering

On the days when I can't remember why I thought being with my children was such a good idea, I dig up an old column by Erma Bombeck. She says of mothering:

> It's a high-risk profession. You win some, you lose some. So why do we do it? It sure isn't the money. I guess it's because I don't know of any other job in the world that brings out the best in people . . . patience, understanding, compassion, strength, selflessness, caring, forgiveness. They are virtues you never knew were within you until you raise a child. I never knew I could say no when my heart wanted so badly to say yes. I never knew I could tell a child the truth when it hurt both of us so much. I never knew I could put anyone above my feelings.

Reading the column again, I think of Janet Lynn, the world champion of women's professional figure skating. An interviewer once asked her how she viewed her role as a mother.

She replied, "I would venture to say I've already experienced what most women are going after in the world as far as fame, fortune, and recognition. I found [the world] to be empty without a higher purpose. . . . And I am grieved for women because I believe that oftentimes women give up the most influential place they will ever have for something that is not going to be so influential or so important. I believe [being a mother] is the most important job—and can be one of the most influential jobs—in the world."

Amen! I agree. Re-motivated, I go back to hemming Nathan's band uniform while I instruct Heidi for the 687th time on why we make our beds in the morning, even though they'll be messed up again twelve hours later.

I need these reminders because there was a time when I wasn't sure kids were worth the bother. In college I'd been influenced by the strident rhetoric of the early women's movement, in which men were nonessential and children merely weights that would hold me back from being all I could be.

The Bible verse I held to was Proverbs 14:4, "Where no oxen are, the manger is clean, but much increase comes by the strength of the ox." I recall thinking to myself, *I'd rather have the clean stall than the oxen's strength.* I was not going to be bothered with children.

When Steve and I married, I thought he understood how adamant I was about a child-free life. Steve, unfortunately, claimed no recollection of ever having talked about it—which only goes to prove that love is deaf and blind, and also a little dense.

However, Steve's grandfather's funeral changed my mind. Seeing this man's extended family, I was struck with the importance of leaving descendants when we die. That same summer at a Basic Youth Conflicts Seminar, Steve and I both heard that in God's plan, children are a blessing. As a result, Steve got a revelation, and I got pregnant.

The morning I was to go for a pregnancy test found me one frightened young woman. How could I ever handle the responsibility of raising a child? What did God think about what was ahead for me?

I went to the Scriptures for direction and began to read. In the first passage I'd randomly selected, I found this thought: "Women will be preserved through the bearing of children." God saw having children as a positive life experience. My attitude would simply have to change. But I knew I couldn't do it myself. I bowed my head and pleaded with Him to calm my fears and stay with me.

Though I had prayed, my fears didn't evaporate and I trudged to the doctor's office. The anxiety must have been evident on my face, because when the nurse told me the tests indicated I was indeed pregnant, she asked, "Would you like to consider an abortion?"

Being faced with the option of getting rid of the baby was just the cold slap I needed. God had created this child to live; surely He would help me as I cared for this little one!

Because loving a child wasn't natural for me, I feel empathy for women who come as slowly as I did to bond with their children. But I also feel some anger toward the anti-mothering rhetoric that almost kept me from the rich life experiences of birthing and raising my children. I can't imagine life without Nathan and Heidi. Without them, my existence would be a lonely vacuum.

## Should Somebody Else Be Raising Our Children?

Fortunately, being pregnant is getting more glamorous. Spiffy maternity shops in the mall are crammed with absolutely great looks worn by mannequins so chic that—except for their rounded bellies—they belong on the pages of *Vogue*.

Television now allows that even smart women become pregnant! A season or two ago on *Wall Street Week* a female regular began showing up in maternity garb, and by season's end had birthed a child. There was even a gentle "mommy" joke or two, done with affection by her pin-striped colleagues, but the jokes didn't detract from the respect she was given as a professional peer.

So now it's hip to give birth. But what still isn't hip is actually staying with these children once they leave the hospital. Television mommies head back to the office, and clever misadventures with the babysitter or the preschool or the bumbling dad get written into the script. In the midst of the chaos, these bright and shiny babies grow up secure, witty, well-mannered, and downright adorable.

A couple of years ago a well-known morning television personality was voted Mother of the Year. Magazine reports explain she has time to do two daily television shows because two full-time nannies care for her children. I could be mother of the year, too, if I never had to be around my kids!

But piecemeal parenting like this isn't God's plan. His mandate to us isn't simply to bring children into the world; it's to disciple them as His people, to *bring them up* in the nurture and admonition of the Lord. Jesus set a model for how to do this when He set out to bring His twelve disciples to spiritual maturity. He didn't disciple His spiritual children by sending them off to seminary for three years. Instead, the scripture says, "He appointed twelve—designating them apostles—*that they might be with Him* and that He might send them out to preach" (Mark 3:14, emphasis mine). If Jesus needed time with His disciples, I don't believe we can disciple our children without being with them.

This was God's plan from Moses' day. He told the children of Israel, "These commandments that I give you today are to be upon your hearts. Impress them on your children. Talk about them when you sit at home and when you walk along the road, when you lie down and when you get up" (Deuteronomy 6:6, 7). This is involved parenting. It means teaching when you're in the checkout line at Wal-Mart, swinging at the park, emptying the potty chair, raking leaves in the backyard. It means being with them. This kind of nurturing is as different from "babysitting" as Mother Teresa is from Madonna. Both names sound like they have something to do with spirituality, but that's where the resemblance stops.

When I see kids with half-active parenting, I think of the sign we saw posted at a motel pool: *Swim at your own risk—no lifeguard on duty!* Christian thinker Elisabeth Elliot said, "It's sobering to me to think that we may be maiming our children by depriving them of normal homelife."

But women are tired of being pushed around; they are quietly coming home to the kids. *U.S. News and World Report* says that the percentage of women in the work force between the ages of twenty and forty-four *dropped* between June and December of 1990, the largest decrease since the early sixties. This drop, which remained unchanged in the first quarter of 1991, seemed significant, economists said, because it appears to be coupled with a change in attitudes.

Nearly thirty percent of working women polled last year said that "wanting to put more energy into being a good homemaker and mother" was a reason to consider giving up work indefinitely—an eleven percent increase over 1989 and the highest such figure in twenty years. And in a survey of 1,000 business professionals, 82% of the women polled said they would choose a career path with flexible full-time work hours and more family time, but slower career advancement over one with inflexible hours and faster advancement. And the number of women who bucked the system and chose to start their own businesses reached an all time high last year of over three million, a fifty percent increase over 1980![1]

My sister Gayle is one of the three million. As a way to make money while she's at home with her own two little ones, she started a day-care she calls "All God's Children." She's licensed by the state of New York and helps her family financially while she shares her mothering skills.

How I admire her! During our early years of parenting, Steve spent two years on the road with a group called Dogwood while I stayed home with Nathan. I sold Avon to earn extra money for curtains, a bedspread, or my make-up. But I also babysat for others, and that work proved to be the hardest way to earn money I've ever attempted! Some of us do these things, though, because we're determined to be with our own kids, even if a price must be paid in the process. It appears the numbers of those who agree with us are growing.

A Chicago executive recruiter said, "We have more women than before who are having second thoughts about giving up everything for a career. When the baby comes along, the six-week maternity leave becomes a two-year maternity leave." And sometimes the work reentry simply never happens.

A musician friend of ours didn't take her child along when she sang on the concert circuit, so they'd had significant separations when he was smaller. When my friend found she was expect-

---

[1] "Trouble at the Top," *U.S. News & World Report*, (June 17, 1991), pp. 42, 44.

ing another child, she talked with the seven-year-old to probe his feelings about their times apart.

"Son," she asked, "if you had to choose between all your nice toys and the things we have, or me staying home here with you, which would you choose?" The boy didn't hesitate. "I would want you home!"

Maybe we are getting smarter. We're learning to say no to those who insist the only jobs worth doing require wearing pantyhose. And we're saying yes to our little ones who need *Mommy's* arms to hold them when they've fallen on the sidewalk, and *Mommy's* values to guide them when the Teenage Mutant Ninja Turtles tell them it's okay to brandish machete knives at those who disagree with you, so long as you throw in an occasional "Yo, Dude" and head for the pizza palace afterwards. We're realizing that others can bathe, feed our kids, or teach them baseball, but it's the way these things are done that will determine who these children become.

## Thinking Through the Stay-At-Home Decision

I personally don't know one woman who says, "I'm going off to work because I can't stand these kids and must get away from them!" Most women who work outside the home do so for one of two reasons: financial pressures, or personal fulfillment.

Some of us have no choice about leaving the children. Either we work away from home, or we don't eat. My friend Linda is like that. Her husband abandoned the family when the children were seven and ten. Linda and the boys wouldn't survive without her income from a clerical job, although she was wrenched at the thought of no longer being there for her sons when they were not in school.

But many of us live in the gray in-between. Our children wouldn't go shoeless if we didn't bring in a paycheck, but it could mean a move to a smaller house, or no piano lessons, or a hundred other changes. These decisions come hard.

In a survey conducted by *Redbook* magazine, 90% of the women they queried said they believed mothers work because they need the money. The question comes, of course: What do we need the money *for*? A nonworking registered nurse from Colorado said, "The majority of the mothers in my neighborhood work, and all claim they couldn't survive financially unless they did. That's true, if they are to pay for their two new cars, big-screen TV, VCR, new home and lush furnishings. . . . I could add a big chunk to our family income, but shouldn't our children realize how important they are? I worked in the Intensive Care Unit for years and made lots of life-and-death decisions, but that job was easy compared with being a parent."

In making such a decision, we need to ask ourselves, *How much money do I need to live the way the Lord wants me to? What kind of price should my family pay for the material lifestyle we live?* Answers to these questions need to be prayerfully considered, because sometimes money costs too much.

The same prayerful consideration must be given as we consider our needs for personal development.

My friend Maureen Rank found that the Lord's leading about her work changed with the seasons in her family's life. While her children were small, it seemed imperative she be with them, even though financial needs would have dictated otherwise. The Ranks cut back their lifestyle so that Mike's income as an auto mechanic could support them. They lived in an old farmhouse, drove secondhand vehicles, filed for reduced-rate school lunches, and learned to make do. Maureen recalls working at home doing freelance book reviews and other writing projects "to help financially and to keep myself from mentally shifting into neutral."

After the kids were older, ages thirteen and nine, a job as a research assistant opened up. The family prayed about it together, and decided to try it for a year. Hours were arranged so Maureen's day started early and ended in time to pick up the kids after school. Not having to watch each nickel and dime so closely proved to be a relief, but the whole family has had to shift to accommodate the shared load of household chores and increased busyness. "It has pluses and minuses," Maureen observes. "Our stability is our confidence that God has led us into this step. We're trusting Him to guide us to keep growing together as a family in the midst of these new pressures and opportunities."

This idea of getting work that will accommodate mothering is the direction my sister Alice chose as well. She purposely sought clerical jobs in the school system so her hours and vacations would coincide with her kids. As her children moved through the system, she moved with them, from elementary, to middle school, then to high school. Now that they've graduated, she works for the Board of Education!

As we seek to answer the question of working alternatives, we need to move cautiously and seek the Lord's will about the answer He has for us. If you're now with your children, be sure the Lord has called you away before choosing to work outside the house. If He has, He'll provide what they need. But if the voice calling you is really that of the world's, you'll be missing a chance at one of the greatest ministries a woman can know, that of investing her life in her little ones.

## Mothering Without Being Smothered

Just because I'm fanatical about the priority of our families doesn't mean I believe Mom needs to be the family slave. We often do far too much for our children. We praise them too much and baby them too much, and spend our lives for them in inappropriate ways that don't actually minister at all.

My position as mother doesn't mean I'm nothing more than a glorified chauffeur. Being a taxi service to a child's 1400 activities is not my idea of having a life. So in our family, each child is allowed one activity outside school hours. Presently for Nathan, it's marching band; for Heidi, gymnastics class. I do not intend to spend my adult years eating burgers in the car on the way from piano lessons to basketball practice.

Besides, children need to know they can't do it all. This, of course, flies in the face of everything America stands for, but I don't care. Kids live stressed, harried lives, hooked on the adrenalin of overachievement because we don't believe they can make it to adulthood without Spanish classes and Art Appreciation and soccer and Library Story Hour and a track meet and kiddie computer class.

We've got to help our kids slow down and learn to live. There are sandpiles to dig in, bicycles to ride, snow forts to construct, and (gasp!) maybe even books to read.

Mothering without being smothered means we *limit what we're willing to do* for our children. It is not in a child's best interest to have a mature, capable adult at his beck and call twenty-four hours a day, waiting to feed him his favorite foods, then clean up his messes, entertain him when he's bored, and pacify him when he's cranky. We're mothers, not handmaidens to royalty.

We also do our kids a great favor when we let them *live with the consequences* of their choices.

Nathan and I used to have verbal knock-down-drag-outs over the issue of his piano practice sessions. I'd put out the money for lessons, then my budding virtuoso wouldn't learn the pieces, and I made life miserable for him.

Finally we talked. In tears, I told him why these lessons mattered so much to me. When I was a little girl, I longed to play the piano, but we could afford neither the piano nor the lessons. So in desperation I took a piece of cardboard, drew a keyboard on it, colored in the black and white keys, and with that taught myself to play.

No wonder it hurt me so when Nathan didn't value the lessons. My son was being given the chance I'd always dreamed of. But it was my own passion for the piano I was feeding, not Nathan's. Once I realized what was happening I abandoned the struggle. "Son," I said, "if you don't practice, that's your choice; but if you don't prepare on your own, I'm no longer paying for the lessons."

This sounded fine to him, and he promptly quit. I may not wind up with a concert pianist, and he may someday regret his choice, but it was time I stopped trying to save him from the consequences of his decision.

Although nothing is harder for us to do, we've got to let our children's ships sink every so often. We'll be wiser and happier mothers if we refuse to protect them from the speed bumps of life, especially those generated from their own foolishness.

I believe our families deserve our best, but they don't deserve our all. We're servants first of Christ, and sometimes serving Christ means refusing to respond to our children's every wish.

# 4

# Evaluating
# Your Mission

# Circles of Influence

I want more from life than to die with my bills paid and a full set of teeth intact. I want God's kingdom to advance and people's lives to be better because I was here.

But how does a country girl from West Virginia change the world? Without power, prestige, or position, how does she make a difference? In the midst of hair to perm, tax papers to file, socks to mend, birthday gifts to buy, children to kiss, and house payments to send off, how does she go about changing the world?

I believe it starts by understanding what it means to change the world. After all, the word "change" can mean many things. You carry change in your purse; the baby's diaper gets changed; Tuesday may be the day you change the beds; we're always changing our minds.

But the kind of change I'm talking about is what Webster describes as "partially or wholly transformed." To me, *partial* is the operative word here. How can I take on the world when most days it's all I can do to get a decent dinner on the table? If I thought I could only fulfill my life's mission by totally changing the world, I would die in despair before I ever found the courage to begin.

But partially transforming some corner of the world—even I can give that a try, with God's help. I believe this is the plan the Lord gave His disciples in Acts 1:8 just before He ascended into heaven.

He said, "You will be my witnesses in Jerusalem, and in all Judea and Samaria, and to the ends of the earth."

Jerusalem was home. They were to start there, and as they saw God using them in Jerusalem, they were to move to the surrounding state, Judea. Then, when God had shown His power to use them in Judea, they were to go on to the rest of the earth.

I call this strategy for a life mission "circles of influence." First the Lord uses me to influence those closest: my husband and children. Then my influence can spread to our extended family and church family. When I've seen His power there, I can venture into the neighborhood, then to the wide arena of my state and nation, and finally to the world.

It isn't God's plan that we begin with a big splash. The changes we effect are a natural outgrowth of being faithful wherever He's planted us. Like the ripples that fan out from a stone thrown into the pond, our influence can spread gradually into wider and wider circles, from very small to very large.

I discovered this ripple effect reading the stories of great women of God: Susanna Wesley, Corrie ten Boom, Catherine Booth, Florence Nightingale. These women changed the world. Their stories moved me to want to do the same. But they also gave me another gift: they showed me the secrets of how such influence grows. From them I learned that the ripple effect happens over the course of a lifetime. And the real magnitude of our impact may not be felt until after we've died. Faithfully serving wherever God planted them was the key to these women's lives. We serve with joy wherever He chooses, and He causes the ripples from our service to spread to the world.

## The First Circle: Our Husband and Children

Our influence in the lives of others begins with God at the center of our own lives, and our living in simple devotion to Him. With His strength and help we can begin to give ourselves in the circle of influence nearest us, our family.

You've probably sung hymns by Charles Wesley hundreds of times: songs like "Hark, the Herald Angels Sing," and "Jesus, Lover of My Soul." But it isn't the sermons of John Wesley, or the songs of Charles Wesley I find so amazing; it's their remarkable mother.

During Susanna's thirty-nine years of marriage, she bore nineteen children, thirteen of whom she lost to death. One daughter was permanently maimed through the carelessness of a nursemaid. Another baby died in the night when a servant girl smothered him.

During much of her married life, the Wesleys served a pastorate in the English countryside. Criminals who had escaped justice lived off the marshlands surrounding the Wesley home and terrorized the family. Even though former clerical families had been driven out of the Elworth parsonage by the bandits, the Wesleys chose to stay.

But many of Susanna's years there were spent alone caring for the children. Her husband fancied himself a poet and a scholar, and therefore felt justified in not giving close attention to family life. His failure to manage their meager income once landed him in debtor's prison, and Susanna lived in constant fear of the bill collector's knock at the door. Once her husband left her for nearly a year after she disagreed with his political views.

Toward the end of the elder Wesley's life, he decided a culmination of it would be a landmark commentary on the Book of Job, so he spent whatever income they could muster on study books. He then closeted himself away for years to write while Susanna managed their home and family. The work was published after his death, but it sold less than five hundred copies and was disparaged by most critics. In the midst of this struggle, the Wesleys lost their home and possessions by fire, and Susanna suffered recurrent illnesses and debilitating depression.

Susanna Wesley's circumstances kept her from reaching very far outside her home. But within those walls, she carried on a ministry to her children that was to change first England, and then the world. In the midst of running the parsonage, conducting the Sunday night church services, and helping to farm the church lands, she schooled all her children herself. She held weekly conferences with each child, and each Thursday night spent two-hour study stretches with John.

As a young woman, Susanna once said, "I hope the fire I start will not only burn all of London, but all of the United Kingdom as well. I hope it will burn all over the world." When she died at age seventy-two, the fire she had begun had indeed reached London and was already going on to change all of England. The fire, of course, came through her sons John and Charles Wesley.

This brave woman makes me want to pray, "Lord, help me change the world through my children." Because of the depth to which Susanna Wesley invested her talent in discipling her children, the history of God's kingdom was rewritten.

When Paul gave Timothy instructions about how the church was to be organized, he said of the man in leadership: "He must manage his own family well and see that his children obey him with proper respect. If anyone does not know how to manage his own family, how can he take care of God's church?" (1 Timothy 3:4, 5). God sees ministering to our families as first priority.

God is not impressed when we run off to deliver beef stroganoff to a church family with a new baby while our own little family dines on canned spaghetti. He's not pleased when we praise the preacher, but fail to show our own husband respect. We earn the right to minister in our church and to the world beyond by first living out godliness at home with those who know us best.

## Touching Our Extended Family and Our Christian Family

Jesus had stern words for those who failed to care for their parents: "Moses said, 'Honor your father and mother,' and 'Anyone who curses his father or mother must be put to death.' But you say that if a man says to his father or mother: 'Whatever help you might otherwise have received from me is Corban' (that is, a gift devoted to God), then you no longer let him do anything for his father or mother. Thus you nullify the word of God . . ." (Mark 7:10–13).

After we've given to our husbands and children, our extended families come next. Concern for this priority is going to affect many of us in the years ahead, and the price for our giving may be high.

Perhaps, like me, you are part of the Sandwich Generation, caring for ailing parents while raising your own children. *Newsweek* magazine reports 40% of those who care for their parents are still raising their own children. The average American woman will spend seventeen years raising children and eighteen years helping aged parents, according to a 1988 U.S. House of Representatives report. And they describe the feelings of it well:

> Anguish, frustration, devotion, and love. A fierce tangle of emotions comes with parenting one's aged parents, and there isn't time to sort out the feelings, let alone make dinner, fold the laundry, and get to work.[1]

The week before I flew to Iowa to meet with my coauthor for work on this book, I made two four-hundred-mile car trips back to West Virginia because my parents needed me. Mother has cancer; Daddy's heart is not strong.

It's no burden to help them, but rather a pleasure to honor two people who've been so generous. I saw my mother join her sisters in caring for their mother after the older woman suffered a stroke, which left her paralyzed and unable to speak for eight years. My mother gave so generously at a time when she was still raising two teenagers, along with caring for Daddy after he'd had a heart attack.

My father showed great love to his aging parents as well. He supported them financially, even while he struggled to make ends meet for his own family.

This is why giving to my parents is one of my deepest satisfactions. But each year the challenge to be helpful grows as my *own* responsibilities require more attention.

---

[1]"Trading Places," *Newsweek,* (July 16, 1990), p. 48.

The church family is a priority as well, and rightly so. Paul says, "As we have opportunity, let us do good to all people, especially to those who belong to the family of believers" (Galatians 6:10).

Service in the church may not seem glamorous, but the effects stretch beyond what we might ever imagine. Back in 1858, a simple Sunday school teacher named Kimball led a Boston shoe clerk to Christ. That clerk was Dwight L. Moody, the great evangelist. During a preaching campaign, Moody challenged Frederick B. Meyer, a pastor of a small church, to reach out with the gospel. Meyer went on to preach on an American college campus, bringing a student named J. Wilbur Chapman to the Lord. Chapman began to minister through the YMCA, and employed a former baseball player named Billy Sunday as an evangelist. Sunday held a revival in Charlotte, North Carolina, which so encouraged a group of local men that they initiated another series of meetings, this time with Mordecai Hamm preaching. During that second revival, a young man named Billy Graham yielded his life to Christ.

Have you ever thought of your simple role as Sunday school teacher with such vision? Humble service in Jesus' name can touch the world.

## Influencing Our Community

Corrie ten Boom's courage in defending the Jews is legendary. But Corrie got involved with the Jews because she was giving herself to her neighborhood. Her family ministered to the retarded and needy in her hometown. Some of these were Jews, so when the Nazis threatened their lives, it was a natural extension of the ten Boom's caring to try to protect their friends. A mission to their neighborhood expanded, eventually touching the world.

As our children began to grow, Steve and I longed to reach out beyond our family to those living around us. Since hospitality seemed a comfortable way for us to begin, we invited our neighbors to a party for Nathan's first birthday. It turned out that the neighbors living on either side of us had never been in each other's houses, or even in the same room during the twenty-five years they'd been living just a few hundred yards apart.

The party was a small start. Next we decided to try finding our way to their hearts through their stomachs. At Christmas I baked an apple pie for the neighbors on each side of us, and delivered them with a note thanking them for being such trustworthy neighbors. Each year thereafter I included two more neighbors, so that last Christmas twenty-six pies and ten dozen cookies went from my kitchen to those living near us.

We decided to reach out to neighborhood children as well. In one venture, we invited them to be part of a home-grown Christmas play called "Is There Room in Your Heart for Him?" The kids acted out the parts and we videotaped it. Later we had a special neighborhood screening for the parents, complete with donuts and hot chocolate.

Other moms in my neighborhood who know the Lord came up with their own idea of ways to touch our area. A new convenience store opened on the corner, a welcome addition to the community—except that it sold pornographic magazines. My two friends organized some thirty neighbors to go together to the market. They called ahead to be sure the manager was there, and appointed Ron a spokesman.

Ron praised the manager for such a clean store. He pointed to the fifteen or so children with the group, and said how they'd looked forward to a place close by to pick up diapers, milk, bread, etc. But because of their concern for their children, they wouldn't be able to shop there because of the destructive influence of those pornographic magazines. Was there anything that could be done?

His orders came from the company's higher-ups, the manager said, and his hands were tied. He was sorry.

"We're sorry, too," Ron said for the group. "We looked forward to the chance to support your business, but of course this conviction is something we can't compromise."

Within a week the magazines were gone.

Two moms made a difference in their neighborhood.

## Changing a Nation

Catherine Booth teamed with her husband William to found the Salvation Army. But she was also part of a lesser known, but perhaps even more courageous stand for right. During the 1800s, the Booths' son, Bramwell, uncovered the widespread practice of selling young English girls into prostitution. Innocent girls were enticed to London. There they were chloroformed, violated, and eventually sent to Paris, Berlin, Rome, or some other city. Many of the victims were as young as thirteen. Even worse, some of the girls were coldbloodedly sold by their parents.

To compound the matter, the violators were protected by law if the girl was at least thirteen. But even if the girl was younger than thirteen, the criminals were still protected, because at that age a girl would not qualify to take an oath or testify.

Catherine Booth boldly joined in the campaign to have the age of consent raised in England so young girls could have legal protection. Catherine spoke at gatherings, stirring sentiment against the evils being perpetrated, and even sought support from Queen Victoria. When a groundswell of support grew, the Booths circulated a petition, and in three weeks garnered nearly 400,000 signatures requesting a change in the laws. When the sheets of signatures were attached to each other, they formed a stream of paper two and a half miles long!

Parliament took notice and eventually passed a law raising the age of consent to sixteen years.

When I read of Catherine Booth's courage, I think of Candy Lightner, whose child was killed by a drunk driver. Instead of shriveling up in grief, Candy channeled her pain into action and founded M.A.D.D. , Mothers Against Drunk Driving. Because of the impact of this coalition, the U.S. now has much stricter laws about driving drunk. Candy Lightner changed her nation.

## Impacting the World

Florence Nightingale grew up in a wealthy home, but chose to forsake her privileged status to serve soldiers in Turkey during the Crimean War. Florence took a crew of thirty-eight nurses with her, and overcoming filth, overcrowding, an appalling scarcity of food and supplies, she went to work. In less than six months she had reduced the hospital death rate from 42% to a little more than 2%.

But her influence only began there. Because her methods were so successful, Nightingale's fame spread throughout the world. She used this platform to fight the opposition of army medical officers and renovate the entire army medical system. In time her ideas on hospital care and nursing spread throughout England and eventually to most of the civilized world.

More than the systems she created, she changed the image of nursing. Before her involvement, nurses were considered women of low reputation. What other kind of woman, after all, would bathe a naked man?

Even worse, nurses cared for soldiers, who in those days were considered the earth's scum. Only the lower class joined the army, and they were thought to be an expendable part of society. This brave woman brought her strength and dignity to those most in need, and changed the way the world thought of and helped the sick.

Influence is meant to have a ripple effect. From a God-centered life, we need to affect first our families, then our church and extended family, then our community, then our nation, then the world.

## When I Think About My World . . .

Nearly two decades ago, Steve and I began singing with a friend named Ron Elder in a little coffeehouse in Nashville. For two years we sang the same songs to the same people each Saturday night. Through serving in this little coffeehouse, we learned the discipline of faithfulness in the place God gave us, and honed the ability to bring fresh insights into old songs.

One night a man approached us and suggested we do a recording. He'd make the arrangements, he said, and pay for the record, so we agreed. Because of this record, a few invitations trickled in from surrounding regions.

In the fall of 1975, someone in Texas came across our record and we were invited to come to their area for two weeks. During that time we sang in Bible studies, coffeehouses, youth meetings, and church services. We counted this Texas trip as the Lord's beginning to extend our influence beyond "Jerusalem," but where it might lead or how it might develop next we didn't know. We knew only that we were to walk through the doors God opened and serve faithfully wherever He led.

Then in 1983, someone sent our record, *Second Honeymoon*, to Dr. James Dobson. As a result, Focus on the Family invited us to sing in a staff chapel service. Steve and I were unspeakably nervous about meeting Dr. Dobson, but we packed up the guitar and went.

That chapel service proved to be God's way of moving us into new circles of influence. The music led to other albums, personal appearances, and the invitation to do a book on marriage.

Now, with over thirteen albums and three books, we marvel at the areas of ministry God has opened up to us. Besides singing and writing, it's our privilege to support pro-life, anti-pornography, and mission groups.

We both know that in these ministries we aren't making great waves that will rearrange the coastline of Christendom; they're still simply quiet ripples. But we're delighted to be part of the kingdom work in the circles the Lord has chosen for us.

We wouldn't have imagined being able to give in all these ways back in the days when we spent every Saturday night in a small coffeehouse in Nashville. Our circles expanded as we continued to give ourselves faithfully in whatever way we could.

What is your mission? How does God want you to be serving your family? Then, in what ways might He want to use you in your church and extended family? Is there a way in your community that you can give of yourself in His name? As you look for answers to these questions, I believe your mission will open up before you just as it did for the women I've told you about, and as it continues to open for us.

Simple devotion to Christ includes an evaluation of three of life's most important investments: marriage, mothering, and mission. But besides evaluating, there are attitudes we need to eliminate if we're to respond to God's call to simple living. And as we eliminate these "albatross attitudes," we can begin to move ahead to establish a lifestyle marked by balance and grace.

# 5

# Eliminating
# Condemnation

# Guilt as Enemy and Friend

Sometimes coming down with a fever can be a positive sign. At least that's how it is for a little boy named Benjamin Stowe.

Eight-year-old Ben underwent a kidney transplant a couple of months ago. In order to keep his body from rejecting its new kidney, the doctors put Ben on a medication that suppresses his immune system. The medicine has a negative side, however. If Ben were to contract a serious disease, his body wouldn't fight back, and he'd likely die.

That's why Ben's fevers are a gift. When his temperature begins to rise, Ben's parents know something is amiss, and rush him to a hospital for the blood work that will indicate what's going on. Then Ben's physicians can adjust the immune-suppressant medication, or provide other treatment to stop the disease's progress. Without the warning sign that his fever provides, Ben's illnesses could become life-threatening before anyone knows enough to intervene.

Guilt is the same kind of gift, a spiritual temperature spike. Guilt makes me miserable, and that discomfort warns me some sin has diseased my spirit. Guilt alerts me to take action against the sin before it spreads and infects my entire life.

## Not Perfect, but Not Condemned

When I start to squirm under the pressure of guilt, I know it's time to reach for God's medicine—by repenting of my sin, then asking for His forgiveness and cleansing.

In this sense, God intended guilt as a friend. But it can also be a powerful and destructive enemy, particularly when I feel guilty for things God has not condemned.

I got blindsided by a tidal wave of this false guilt last week at the grocery store. The episode started innocently enough, with a simple query from the checkout person.

She finished price-scanning my purchases, then asked, "Do you have any coupons?"

Coupons? Of course I didn't have any coupons. In order to have coupons, I would have had to think about what I was going to buy before I came to the store. So here I was, about to be exposed before God and this witness behind the cash register as the slap-dash meal planner that I am. And a wasteful one, at that; I could have paid less for these items, had I diligently clipped, filed, and redeemed the way we frugal homemakers are supposed to.

Under the influence of humiliation I've done some pretty embarrassing things, but this was one of the worst. Instead of covering my tracks with a simple "No coupons today," I started to babble.

"I know I should use coupons," I said hurriedly. "I just read an article about a woman who saved enough by couponing to buy a new house! But if you knew what my week has been like . . . well . . . I haven't had time to read the paper, or actually even SEE the paper. . . ."

By now the checkout person was looking at me as if I were a certified nut case. "Look, lady," she interrupted, "I've got problems of my own. Maybe you should just move along."

I grabbed the grocery bag and slunk out of the store.

My couponless lifestyle isn't all I feel guilty about. There's also the matter of exercise.

We all know it's impossible to be a useful member of Western civilization without having a consistent exercise program. The lack of exercise doesn't just mean you are not fit—it means you're a misfit, nothing less. And a misfit is what I am doomed to be because I cannot seem to get regular at this exercise thing.

To make matters worse, I live with a jogger so disciplined he makes the mail carriers and their "neither wind nor rain nor sleet nor dark of night" pledge look like slackers in comparison. He simply does not miss a scheduled run. And he's pommeled his body into such enviable condition that he has run marathons. I, on the other hand, puff along with my thighs flapping in the breeze, cellulite bouncing as I go.

My flab-induced guilt pushed me into buying exercise gizmos I've barely touched. Nathan now uses my mini-trampoline rebounder to dunk basketballs. My stationary bike, at last count, had accumulated four or five layers of dust.

My latest acquisition was a nifty motorized treadmill. I convinced Steve this was finally the key to wooing me into a lifetime of exercise. I groveled to get him to agree to buy it, but alas, the only consistent action it sees is when I use the handlebars as a drying rack for hand-washables.

I did find one moment of comfort in a report in *USA Weekend*. Readers told what *they* had done with their exercise equipment. Most had me beat for creativity.

One man recycled the idle balance beam he had given his wife into the main support for a new wooden deck he built onto the back of their home. Lavender barbells have become quite serviceable bookends for a woman from California. But exercise bikes seemed to find the most intriguing secondary uses. A Kansas woman uses hers to keep the broken door of her clothes dryer closed. "Our bike," a Nebraska couple said dryly, "is exercising its right to be called stationary."

These confessions tell me I'm not the only well-intentioned exercise slug on the planet. Still, my lack of discipline embarrasses me. This embarrassment *feels* like the guilt that God invokes when He's trying to convict me of some sin. By

not exercising, I've failed to meet my own expectations. When I grocery shop without coupons, I
fail to meet what I think others expect of me. In
both cases I haven't measured up to someone's
standards; I've fallen short. But I don't believe in
either case I've "fallen short of the glory of God,"
as the Bible describes sin in Romans 3:23.

A while back I saw a bumper sticker that read,
"Life is short. Eat dessert first." Though pigging
out on dessert isn't wise dieting advice, I liked
the slogan. To me it said, "Lighten up." Homes
will not break up, children will not go to bed hun-
gry, and the sun will not fall from the sky if I miss
double-coupon day or fail to get my thighs in
shape. We've got to keep touch with reality. God
wants us to be obedient, not obsessive. *Living simply* means concentrating on what's important in
light of eternity, and not taking the rest of life too
seriously.

## When Our Wrongs Deserve All the Attention We Can Muster

Wasting our spiritual sensitivity on coupon redemption can distract us from seeing a much
larger issue: that of our total depravity before
God.

A few months ago, Steve and I sang for a conference at which Rebecca Pippert spoke about
grace. There she told this story:

Several years before, a broken young woman
had confessed to Becky Pippert that she'd
aborted her unborn child. The girl and her boy-

friend were respected youth leaders in a conservative church, so when she became pregnant out of wedlock, neither could face the humiliation of telling their church. They decided to abort the baby.

The young woman said weeping, "My wedding day was the worst day of my entire life. Everyone in the church was smiling at me, thinking me a bride beaming in innocence. But do you know what was going through my head as I walked down the aisle? All I could think to myself was, *You're a murderer. You were so proud that you couldn't bear the shame and humiliation of being exposed for what you are. But I know what you are, and so does God. You have murdered an innocent baby.*"

She went on, "I just can't believe I could do something so horrible. How could I have murdered an innocent life? How is it possible I could do such thing? I love my husband; we have four beautiful children. I know the Bible says that God forgives all of our sins. But I can't forgive myself! The thought that haunts me the most is *how* could I murder an innocent life?"

Becky Pippert's response shocked me. She said to the girl, "I don't know why you're so surprised. All of us are responsible for the death of the only innocent who ever lived. Jesus died for all of our sins. The very sin of pride that caused you to destroy your child is what killed Christ as well. If you have done it before, then why couldn't you do it again?"

The girl understood immediately. She had done something much worse than killing her baby. Her sin drove Jesus to the cross. Then she said, "If the cross shows me that I am far worse than I had ever imagined, it also shows me that my evil has been absorbed and forgiven. If the worst thing any human can do is to kill God's Son, and if *that* can be forgiven, then how can anything else—even my abortion—not be forgiven?"

The truth is, we are hopelessly decadent sinners, bent on evil in every cell of our being. We laughed at redemption and sent the Redeemer to His death. But God took the blood His beloved Son shed on the cross and washed away the stain of our sin. Becky Pippert says, "What God reveals through the cross is that we are far worse than we ever imagined, and yet forgiveness is offered to us."[1]

Godly guilt pierces me, and leads me to repentance and freedom. But when guilt, like a fever, hangs on and on, danger lies ahead. Guilt over things God doesn't consider essential can bind me with chains of worthlessness and despair, and keep me from moving forward in God's joy.

The Lord offers encouragement from 1 John 3:19–21: "We set our hearts at rest in his presence whenever our hearts condemn us. For God is greater than our hearts, and he knows everything. Dear friends, if our hearts do not condemn us, we have confidence before God. . . ."

---

[1]Rebecca Pippert, *Hope Has Its Reasons* (San Francisco: Harper & Row, 1991), pp. 103, 104.

## Learning Endurance

We all have different arenas in which we struggle against Satan's accusations. The Bible tells us that he berates us day and night before the Father's throne, so we should expect harassment from time to time. The difficulty for me comes in discerning when it's the Devil's harassment, as opposed to God convicting me of sin. The place I most often face this challenge of discernment is when I'm feeling fat.

Nothing makes me feel more condemned than going off my diet. Like many women, dieting has become my unpaid vocation. I will know I've gone to heaven when I can eat at the Marriage Feast of the Lamb and not have to count calories!

I recall the exact day when my vague sense of "not-all-right-ness" about my appearance became a force I knew I'd have to reckon with. On January 30, 1987, Steve and I sang for the opening of the Focus on the Family headquarters in Pamona, California. Seated on the platform, I looked around at the other women. They looked to be size 5, 6, 7 . . . whew! Was I intimidated! You could have added a couple of those together and still not quite come up with my dress size. Even Chuck Colson had lost weight, and looked positively svelte. I'd had dieting success at various intervals in my life (I've lost seven or eight hundred pounds over the years . . . and gained them all back eventually.) At that moment, though, I was thirty-five pounds heavier than I am now, and I felt like a porker.

Something had to give so I could feel peace in place of chagrin. Either those pounds had to go or I was going to have to have a major attitude transplant so I could accept myself at my present weight.

I knew how I felt about those extra pounds. But a more important question needed answering before I chose a plan of action. What did God think? Was the disgust I felt a probe from the Holy Spirit to convict me of the sin of gluttony, or was it simply false guilt?

One thing I knew: hearing God's voice would take some careful listening on my part, because the world had brainwashed me into thinking unless my tummy was Fonda-flat, I couldn't be worth much. And that message is wrong.

For one thing, the models we see on television aren't models at all. They're a facsimile of the truth—an illusion—because they give the impression that thinness doesn't require discipline. If television depicted reality, Tom Selleck would invite a beautiful woman to dinner, and she'd order two spinach leaves and a boiled egg— hold the yolk. Instead, she stuffs herself on chateaubriand at 262 grams of fat per serving, and 465-calorie-a-glass wine, yet goes home the size she came.

If models do add poundage, they get it sucked out, lifted up, tucked in, or cut off. Or if they diet, they don't also have to make brownies for Little League, or serve macaroni and cheese for dinner because shrimp isn't in the budget. The point is, they can't be models *for me* because they don't live life as I know it. Yet I let their image dictate how I feel I should look.

Where did we get this "you can't be too thin" definition of beauty, anyway? A century ago, Nancy Reagan would have been considered emaciated and deserving of our pity. Beauties had rounded hips and fleshy thighs. Sizes 14 or 16 or more would have been desirable, because culture defined attractiveness differently. As I once told Steve, "I may not have a weight problem at all. I was simply born a hundred years too late!"

Meeting cultural expectations of beauty can sometimes bring me to the point of silliness. I know you've seen the *National Geographic* magazines with pictures of people who put wooden plugs in their ears to stretch the lobe until it hangs down to their waist. I used to shake my head at what I considered ignorant barbarism, until I thought of the women in our country today who are emaciating themselves through anorexia and bulimia, simply because someone has convinced them you can never be too thin.

I remember Erma Bombeck telling about the woman who for years had been starved in a Japanese POW camp. Her rescuers carried her skin-and-bones frame to a hospital, and as they lifted her onto a scale, she suddenly came to life and began to scream, "Only four more pounds and I'll be at my goal weight!"

With all these false messages fogging my brain, it was no wonder I had difficulty knowing what God thought about my weight. So I asked Him to speak to me, and to lead His lamb like the wise and faithful Shepherd He is.

His answer came in part through a conversation with a friend. "Annie," she confessed one day, "there has never been a day in my whole life when I didn't wake up hating myself for the way I look."

I was stunned. This intelligent, charming, successful woman loathed herself because of thirty extra pounds!

"Louise," I responded, "you know I think you're lovely. But if the pounds bother you so much, why don't you lose them?"

Her response showed she knew how to be completely honest with herself. "I don't lose weight because I know hitting my goal wouldn't be the end of struggle; it'd be just the beginning. With the way I'm put together, it would require a daily fight for the rest of my life to maintain the figure I'd like to have. I guess I don't want to begin a war I'll never be able to finish. It's easier not to battle at all."

As I drove home from the restaurant, I thought about the well-known "Serenity Prayer," adapted from Dr. Reinhold Niebuhr: "God, grant me the serenity to accept the things I cannot change; the courage to change the things I can, and the wisdom to know the difference." I could change how much I weighed. Maybe I couldn't change it in a week, and surely I couldn't change it without expending major energy, but I could change. Perhaps God wanted me to trust Him for the courage to begin the fight against fat.

However, my friend helped me to see something I couldn't change. Even if I finally got into a size 7, there would never be a time when it would be easy to stay there, given my particular body and emotional make-up. God wanted me to persevere in the struggle against those extra pounds, but at the same time He seemed to be telling me to *accept* my physical and emotional temperament that makes weight-loss difficult. Indeed, maybe I was even to be thankful for such a temperament.

Hebrews 10:36 came to mind: "You have need of endurance, so that when you have done the will of God, you may receive what was promised." I need endurance to fulfill God's will for me. Persevering in a struggle against overweight could toughen me as a soldier in the kingdom army.

These thoughts turned out to be God's answer to my prayer for direction. With God's help, I have lost weight—and gained some back and lost it, gained again and lost, then gained . . . if you've dieted at all, you understand the process.

But He's also graced me with acceptance of the struggle. A few months ago a magazine interviewer asked me what I'd like to change about myself if I could. My answer surprised both of us. What I'd change is the one thing I wouldn't. Naturally, I'd love to exchange my body for one that refused to gain weight. I get tired of the focus food has to be for me. But this struggle for slimness is teaching me to endure hardship, so in one sense, I welcome it. I've learned to savor victories, to seek God's grace after failure, and to pick myself up and go on toward obedient living. I no longer expect perfection of myself, simply endurance.

I've taken this lesson about food and begun applying it to exercise. Though I'll never join Steve in those marathons, I do want to be more fit, and I believe God wants this for me as well. So I've finally plugged in the motorized treadmill. Even if my huffing doesn't produce perfect muscle tone, I sense the smile of God as I work at endurance.

# 6

# Eliminating Covetousness

# Guess Who's Coming to Dinner?

The day started out like any other. Little did I know that by its end I would be well on my way to breaking one of the Ten Commandments.

When my pastor's wife handed me the names of the three other couples on our "supper club" list, I eagerly looked to see whom Steve and I would be spending an evening a month with for the next four months. It was going to be such fun! We attend a large church, so getting to know other couples can be difficult. The "supper club" was a way for couples to begin what we hoped would be a long-term friendship.

As I looked over the names, my heart sank. The first couple on my list was the last I would have picked. I hadn't met them, but their home was so magnificent a photographer had used it as a setting for one of our album covers.

That house was indelibly impressed in my mind—6,500 square feet of luxury, complete with a tennis court, swimming pool, and Mercedes in the driveway. And the owners of *that* house were now coming to *my* house for dinner.

Suddenly this cozy little place with the country kitchen and touches of West Virginia memorabilia no longer looked warm and charming to me. Instead, it bordered on tacky. As I thought about it, my palms got sweaty and I felt sick to my stomach. Was it too late for a complete renovation? I wondered what a professional interior decorator would cost.

Steve made it clear no decorator would be in the offing. He was disgusted to think I'd want to change the house to please someone else. The checkbook would not be available to support such a silly venture. I knew then I'd have to ride out this terror on my own.

I did weasel Steve into letting me get new priscilla curtains for the kitchen, because one of the kids had, in a fit of artistic energy, redecorated the old ones with a permanent felt-tip marker. And how I cleaned! Everything was scrutinized and sanitized, including closets and dresser drawers. I was truly paranoid about appearing inferior; did I really think that between courses our guests were going to excuse themselves and take to snooping in our dressers?

My insecurity didn't stop with the house. Choosing an entree terrified me as well. Then there was the matter of the dishes on which I'd serve the meal. Steve and I were bona fide keep-only-the-worldly-goods-you-can-carry-in-a-backpack hippies when we married. In hippiedom, you simply were not on a wedding registry for crystal and fine china. We'd have broken the Hippie Code of Ethics. Consequently, my good dishes (in fact, my *only* dishes) are a simple brown stoneware. Which suited me fine—until I began to cower in the face of the "rich folks' invasion."

In life's vicious game to have the shiniest stuff, I was losing badly. Then one day as I sat stewing over menus and table settings, a quiet voice whispered to my heart.

*Annie, thou shalt not covet. . . .*

What? What was that?

*I said, "Thou shalt not covet. . . ."*

Often when a quiet thought strikes me as did this one, I assume God may be speaking. But atmospheric conditions must have been goofing up the cosmos and causing God's message to misbeam, because this surely couldn't be a word for me. I'm quick to admit I fall prey to a number of sins, but covetousness isn't among them. Why, I'm just a simple country girl from the West Virginia hills. Coveting is a sin practiced by Hollywood starlets; by those diamond-doused women I see at the mall. Not me! It wasn't *coveting* that was making me so upset. It was more like, well, wishful thinking or longing admiration.

But God seemed unconvinced.

*Thou, even thou, West Virginia farm girl, thou shalt not covet. . . .*

This was getting annoying, so I decided to go straight to the source and look up the Ten Commandments. It was as I remembered: "You shall not covet your neighbor's wife. . . ." Coveting is pretty terrible when it involves adulterous acts or thoughts, but I wasn't lusting after anyone who didn't belong to me. Prettier dishes were all I wanted.

*Read it again.*

"You shall not covet your neighbor's house. You shall not covet your neighbor's wife, or his manservant or maidservant, his ox or donkey, or anything that belongs to your neighbor" (Exodus 20:17).

I was beginning to squirm. Could it be these feelings I'd excused as an "inferiority complex" and "low self-esteem" were actually covetousness? My neighbor's house was obviously a problem for me. And their cleaning lady. And nanny. They had no ox or donkey for transportation, but the Mercedes they did have provoked me nicely.

As I began to listen, and mull over the meaning of this tenth commandment, several things about the evil inherent in covetousness began to come clear to me.

## Coveting Insults God's Generosity

Nothing angers me more than to have worked hard at finding the perfect gift for my children, only to have them whine that what they really wanted was something else.

After David's sin with Bathsheba, when the prophet Nathan delivered God's rebuke, he said this: "The Lord God of Israel says, 'I made you king of Israel and saved you from the power of Saul. I gave you his palace and his wives and the kingdom of Israel and Judah; and if that had not been enough, I would have given you much, much more. Why then have you . . . done this horrible deed?' " (2 Samuel 12:7–9).

The cry I hear comes not from an angry judge, but from the heart of a wounded parent. God had inundated David's life with remarkable women— first the princess Michel, then the intelligent and beautiful Abigail, then all of Saul's wives and concubines. And God says He would have gone on to give more had David only sought Him, or had God seen that it was not enough!

But David chose to spit on God's generosity. Instead of being overwhelmed with gratitude for the lavish gifts God had bestowed, he said, "I want MORE, and the MORE I must have is what you've given my neighbor."

No wonder God bled, and punished David so severely.

I've always viewed David's great offense with Bathsheba as that of adultery and murder—and indeed, these are abominable sins. But as I read God's response to David, I've come to wonder if covetousness was the more heinous sin, the root cause of the other sins.

## Coveting Thrives on SELF-Centeredness

As I mentally played back a recording of my anxious thoughts about the upcoming supper club I heard this:

"I am so worried about how I am going to look. Will they think I am a terrible decorator? Will I feel inadequate when they see what I have prepared? I'm afraid that I will be looked down upon, and I. . . ."

Obviously the key word here was "I."

Coveting turned my attention totally to me— *my* needs, *my* appearance, *my* self-esteem. No wonder God hates it! And no wonder that one of His antidotes for covetousness is giving. The book of Proverbs says this: "He [the covetous] is greedy to get, while the godly love to give" (Proverbs 21:26).

A wealthy friend of mine told of the time she wore her mink coat to Bible study. When she walked in the door, her husband hissed, "*Why did you wear that?*" None of the other couples had means to buy such a coat, and the wealthier couple were conscious of not making anyone feel uncomfortable. My friend, however, had come directly from a luncheon and hadn't thought about the statement the coat might make to those in the study. At her husband's comment, she quickly slipped the coat off and folded it inside out so that only the lining showed.

But the coat hadn't gone unnoticed. Later in the evening, my friend went to use the restroom. When she came out, she was face-to-face with another woman in the study who glared at her and said coldly, "*I hate rich people.*"

Another time, my friend became acquainted with one of the mothers while they worked together in the church nursery. How delighted she was when the woman said, "I enjoy your friendship so much, I'd love to have you and your family over for dinner."

But the pleasure of the moment was short-lived. The following week, the hostess-to-be withdrew her invitation. "I found out this week how much money you have," she explained, "and I can't possibly have you in my home because it isn't nearly as nice as yours."

What pain my friend experienced in these two encounters! She'd been piercingly rejected simply on the basis of her financial status; who she was as a person was not taken into consideration. And though she has been treated with the rudest unkindness, those who wounded her no doubt felt they had every right to their behavior, simply because she had money.

## Covetousness Emphasizes the Temporal and Ignores the Eternal

Covetousness pushes us to act as if the singer Madonna were right . . . we really are nothing more than "material girls, living in a material world." But it simply isn't true.

Jesus said, "Watch out! Be on your guard against all kinds of greed; a man's life does not consist in the abundance of his possessions" (Luke 12:15).

Under any circumstance, it's difficult to distinguish what will last from what will not. Often temporal success looks very important; it shouts to be chosen. A promotion at work may look wonderful and pay better, but those new responsibilities might demand more of you than you can give. The advancement may be a "wolf in sheep's clothing," and wind up devouring you or your family life.

Barbara Bush understood this, and spoke with an eye to the eternal when she told the women of Wellesley College, "Cherish your human connections, your relationships with family and friends . . . those human connections with spouse, with children, with friends are the most important investment you will ever make. At the end of your life, you will never regret not passing one more test, winning one more verdict, or closing one more deal. You will regret time not spent with a husband, a child, a friend, or a parent."

Diapering a baby is an eternal act that looks temporary. In that moment when a parent is leaning over their baby, and their eyes lock in a steady gaze, true bonding occurs. Parent/child intimacy doesn't spring up according to scheduled fifteen-minute intervals. It happens at 2:00 A.M. when your eyes are bloodshot and feel like they're full of gravel. In those unplanned moments, heaven hushes while a parent and child are suspended in a loving eye-to-eye embrace. It didn't feel eternal when you crawled out of bed, but it was.

Discerning what is eternal isn't easy; it is often camouflaged in the simple, ordinary things of life. The temporal is brassy and demanding and loud. It stands up and screams for our attention. But we have to train our eyes to see the eternal in the unlikely events of everyday life.

I believe seeing the eternal means choosing to play ball while the supper dishes wait, or putting down that book you've been reading and turning over to talk to your husband.

But covetousness clutters our way with stumbling-blocks as we walk toward the eternal. Perhaps that's why the Bible so firmly admonishes, "Do not love the world or anything in the world. . . . For everything in the world—the cravings of sinful man, the lust of the eyes and the boasting of what he has and does—comes not from the Father, but from the world. The world and its desires pass away, but the man who does the will of God lives forever" (1 John 2:15–17).

These verses give a clear focus on eternity, but it's a focus we simply can't maintain when we're busy wanting what someone else has.

## Covetousness Means We Reject God's Plan for Our Lives

We were made to be just what we need to be to fill the place of service God designed for us. The Book of Esther illustrates this principle beautifully.

Esther was a Jewish captive in the land of the Medes and the Persians. King Xerxes chose her above all the women in the land to be his queen. In order to ready herself to appear before the king, Esther was treated to a twelve-month beauty makeover. Six months with oil and myrrh, the scripture says, then six months with perfumes and cosmetics. Although this isn't a beauty regimen I've ever seen chronicled in the pages of *Glamour* magazine, it certainly must have worked. When Esther finally went before the king, she won the favor of everyone who saw her, and the King's heart as well.

Her appointment to the throne put her in just the position of power the Lord could use in the years ahead. When Haman, a wicked government official, hatched a plan to destroy the Jews held captive in Persia, Esther courageously interceded for her people. She made good use of the tools she'd been given. Dressed in her royal robes, her stunning appearance pleased the king. She must have also known how to put on a smashing dinner party, because her next tactic was to invite the king to dine. He was so enchanted with her hospitality that he promised to fulfill any request, up to half his kingdom. At that moment, Esther was able to do what an invading army could not have done. She asked for, and was given, the spared lives of God's people.

For Esther to fulfill God's plan took courage and faith. But Esther's beauty, poise, and gracious hospitality were necessary as well. The Lord knew just what she needed to serve Him, and He saw to it she was equipped and in the right place to save the nation.

Harriet Tubman, on the other hand, likely could not have filled God's place for her if she had been a physically beautiful woman. Born a plantation slave, Harriet grew up to play a significant part in the Underground Railroad. Almost singlehandedly she led more than three hundred slaves to freedom, and served as a Yankee spy in the Civil War.

Like Esther, Harriet exuded courage and faith. And like Esther, she was physically fitted for the role she'd play. By the time she was fifteen, grueling work in the fields had muscled her like a man. Visitors to the plantation would marvel at the stocky young girl who could lift huge hogsheads and pull a loaded wagon like an ox.

During that fifteenth year, Harriet stood between a plantation owner and a runaway slave. Furious at her insolence, the owner grabbed a two-pound iron weight and hurled it at Harriet, striking her in the forehead and fracturing her skull. Although she survived, she suffered a large dent in her forehead, causing pressure on her brain that resulted in unpredictable sleeping spells, which would be with her the rest of her life.

The injuries worked to her advantage, however. She looked coarse, and frightened people when they found her standing fast asleep, holding her broom. Sometimes she'd drop off to sleep in the middle of a sentence. Her master concluded he had a worthless piece of merchandise on his hands. As a last-ditch attempt to get some return from her, he decided to let her find work on other plantations as she was able. This punishment gave Harriet the freedom she needed to at last connect to the Underground Railroad. And as a railroad "conductor," she often dressed as a wizened old woman, or even a man, to avoid detection. With her rough features and burly body, the authorities never caught on.

Had Esther and Harriet Tubman exchanged physical appearances, neither could have filled the place God had for them. The same is true for us—physically, financially, emotionally, relationally, intellectually. Before we were born, God fitted us for our place in His plan. If we waste our time coveting what He's given another, we're saying we don't like His plan, and we'll miss the joy of living out the particular and perfect plan for which we were created.

I think often of Solomon's prayer: "Give me neither poverty nor riches, feed me with the food that is my portion" (Proverbs 30:8, NASB).

That's what I want: to have just what is needful for me, no more, no less. I don't want someone else's portion, just my own, so I can bring God joy in filling the place where He wants to use me.

## Longings Aren't Wrong If They Pull Us on Toward God

Sometimes we fall into the trap of thinking our desires in themselves are wrong. But it's not our longings that are evil; it's what we do with them.

Even as David contemplated taking Bathsheba, the Lord did not condemn his longing. He condemned the taking of what was not his. God knows we are spiritual beings and that even the best of His earthly gifts, be they partners or palaces, in the end will not satisfy us. Deep in our innermost being lies a passionate, unquenchable longing for Him, which will only know consummation in heaven.

Our great mistake comes not in feeling incomplete, but in looking to our neighbor's stuff to fill the void, rather than looking to God. In fact, our longings can turn us to God in new and deeper ways. Coveting turns us away from Him, from seeking more of the Giver to grabbing for more of His gifts. His gifts were given for us to enjoy, but if we expect them to fill His place in our lives, we are expecting something they simply can't do, and as a result we'll sacrifice any enjoyment we could have derived from them.

That's why the Lord admonishes us, "Keep your lives free from the love of money, and be content with what you have, because God has said, 'Never will I leave you; never will I forsake you' " (Hebrews 13:5).

## Getting My Just Desserts

All this ballyhoo over covetousness wasn't lost on me. When I quit justifying myself, and called my sin what it was, the Lord graciously forgave me. And I soon found my focus began to change from how I could be known as the "great entertainer" to how I could show genuine hospitality to my brothers and sisters.

With the pressure off, I relaxed, and envisioned a friendly and noncompetitive atmosphere. I had a simple menu, so I could visit instead of fuss in the kitchen; in fact, I even wound up serving cookies and ice cream for dessert. And of course we had a delightful evening, and began some friendships we hope will grow in the years ahead.

As it turned out, the wealthy couple I had so feared were two of the most down-to-earth people we'd met in a long time. They helped make the evening a genuine pleasure for all of us. In fact, later I was comfortable enough to confess to the woman how intimidated I felt about having her in my home. She responded with such grace that I wound up laughing at the silliness of it. She laughed, too, at the image I'd concocted of her; when her turn came to host the supper club, she planned to have us eat from paper plates!

# 7

# Eliminating Cursing

# For Bitter or Better

Eighty years ago, the largest and most luxurious ocean liner ever built set out on her maiden voyage. Dignitaries smashed champagne bottles against her hull, English crowds cheered, and newspapers trumpeted the launching of the ship that couldn't go down.

Eleven days later, the *Titanic* lay at the bottom of the North Atlantic.

The sea of life teems with icebergs just waiting to sink our ship. Sometimes, those who seem as unsinkable as the *Titanic* are lost. Others run into the same obstacles, yet manage to steam safely into the harbor.

I believe the difference is one of attitude. Unsinkable people have been fortified with *the ability to forgive* the hurts life brings.

After the death of her little son, Anne Morrow Lindbergh wrote, "I do not believe that sheer suffering teaches. If suffering alone taught, all the world would be wise, since everyone suffers."

How we respond to life's difficulties makes the difference.

Learning to respond to suffering has led me to the life of Joseph. This young Israelite started out as his father's pet. But a pit and a prison stood in the way of his place in the royal palace. This young man's response to the wounds others inflicted upon him provides the model I need to strengthen me when I've crashed into an iceberg once again.

## Joseph Finds Himself in the Pits

Joseph was number eleven in a family of twelve sons. His father adored him, his brothers did not.

Sibling rivalry rears its ugly head in most families. It certainly did in ours.

I was the fourth of six children. My birth was intended to be the last, since I completed the scenario my mother had envisioned for her family— two boys, two girls. But when I was seven Becky came along, to the surprise of my parents. Two years later, Gayle joined us. Because I was the youngest of the oldest "gang" of children, I was often put in charge of the two little ones.

I loved my baby sisters, but kids can be loving and cruel to each other at the same time. And so was I. Making them cry gave a feeling of superiority, so I worked at finding which buttons to push to put them in a tizzy. Name-calling seemed to work best, so as often as I could get away with it, I taunted them with "Ugly Toad" and "Pig

Wart." They'd get mad and cry, and I'd get my thrill for the day.

And so it went—until they were old enough to figure out what revenge was. They'd grab the broom and chase me around the house. When they got me cornered—crack! I'd get smacked right across the shins with the wooden handle.

Our mother didn't interfere; she'd given up trying to act as referee. Life at our house definitely became survival of the fittest.

But even though there were days when we probably made the James Gang look like Boy Scouts, we never attempted anything lethal on each other.

Not so with Joseph's brothers. When they spotted him coming to meet them in the field, they hatched a plan to rid themselves of him. They'd kill him, then throw his body in a pit and claim a wild animal was responsible.

Joseph's only salvation came from his brother Reuben, who talked the others into simply throwing him into the pit and letting him die of natural causes. This sounded agreeable . . . why dirty their hands on Joseph's account? He wasn't worth it. So into the pit Joseph was cast, and his brothers sat down to dinner.

As they ate, a caravan of Ishmaelite slave traders bound for Egypt happened by. At once the brothers' sadistic minds realized this was their chance—they could get rid of Joseph, and make a profit besides. They sold him to the slavers for the equivalent of $12.80.

History tells us Joseph's pit was actually a dry cistern hewn from solid rock. These were often made narrower at the mouth than at the base, so it would be almost impossible to escape without help.

Often people feel as though they are trapped in a pit from which there is no escape. Maybe your pit was childhood abuse or abandonment. Others grapple with singleness, divorce, childlessness, or an empty nest. Disease can invade our lives, or we may be faced with a child's illness or rebellion, a husband's infidelity or death. Maybe your pit is financial worry or depression.

Whatever it is, you may identify with the despair Joseph felt when trapped in that pit. What Joseph didn't know was that his fall into the pit was the first step of a journey that would bring him to the palace. The pit wasn't the end of his life; it was the beginning. So it can be for you, with God's help.

## From the Pit to Potiphar's House

In the life of Joseph—scene two—Potiphar, the captain of Pharaoh's guard, bought Joseph from the traders, and the young man became a household slave.

What would you or I have felt at this point, had we been Joseph? In just a few weeks the life of this seventeen-year-old boy was completely turned around—from favored son to palace slave, from a life in control to no control at all. He could have understandably crawled into a corner, curled into a fetal position, and proceeded to die of self-pity. He could have done what he was forced to do, and nothing more, letting those around him know how unjustly life had treated him.

But he didn't do either of these.

Even though Joseph had been victimized, he didn't react like a victim. Instead, he began to serve aggressively with the skills he'd been given. The scripture says, "When his master saw that the Lord was with him and that the Lord gave him success in everything he did, Joseph found favor in his eyes and became his attendant. Potiphar put him in charge of his household, and he entrusted to his care everything he owned" (Genesis 39:3, 4).

We have all been victimized in one way or another. If statistics hold true, one of four women has been sexually abused by the time she is eighteen. From my conversations with women, I'd estimate the percentage to be higher than that. Emotional abuse can come from many sources: unloving parents, an angry spouse, selfish children, manipulative friends, dishonest business associates. We are victims whenever we suffer because of the choices others have made.

But we cease being the victim when we expose our pain to God. He wants us to be honest and open with Him. Hiding our hurts under the guise that "a Christian shouldn't feel this way" simply doesn't work. We're not fooling the Lord, and we're not honoring Him by assuming He isn't strong enough to receive our hurt and rage without wilting or retaliating.

Have you ever gone toe-to-toe with God and made an honest appraisal of the things in life you most resent? Have you ever asked Him where He was when you were being taken advantage of? Have you ever let yourself cry out, "Why did you allow this to happen to me?"

Those who love God most seem to fight with Him more ferociously. Rest assured, God is strong enough not to be decimated by your anger, or shocked by your sin, or terrified by your accusations. David said, "O people, pour out your hearts to him . . ." (Psalm 62:8). We can pound our angry fists against His chest, because all the while His strong arms are holding us, and He will never push us away.

It could be that you were the victimizer, not the victim. Maybe you aborted your baby or abused your child, have been unfaithful in your marriage, or brought great pain to others by selfish choices. If any of this is true in your life, you must resist the temptation to take care of your sins in your own way. Only God can forgive and cleanse us of all sin.

I once talked with a young woman who was bent on abusing herself. She'd break bones, draw blood, pull out her hair. Though I'm not a psychiatrist, it seemed to me she was trying to pay the penalty for her many sins herself.

We cannot atone for our sins. If we could, Christ would not have had to die on the cross. Instead of trying to free ourselves of guilt, we must give that guilt up to God, and repent of the evil in our hearts. Once we admit our sin, He can cleanse us, and fill our hearts with peace.

I believe the anchor of Joseph's life was his faith in God's sovereign control. He truly believed God was not surprised by what happened in his life, and the apparent evil that had befallen him was part of God's plan. Because Joseph trusted God's control, he could in turn take control of Potiphar's household, and even of his own passions.

Controlling his desires proved to be a valuable discipline for Joseph. Not only was Potiphar pleased with Joseph, but so was Potiphar's wife.

The story has all the makings of a soap-opera script: "Now Joseph was well-built and handsome, and after a while his master's wife took notice of Joseph and said, 'Come to bed with me!' " (Genesis 39:6, 7).

Joseph resisted the woman's seductive advance. Day after day he persisted in pushing her away. His courage to resist temptation emphasizes the fact that he had resolved with God any bitterness he felt about his captivity. Otherwise, Joseph could have rationalized the many reasons for succumbing to the temptation put before him. He had just lost his homeland, he was separated from his beloved father and younger brother, his culture, his religious practices, his language, his inheritance, and his freedom. His heart surely must have been broken with grief, and he must have been intensely lonely at times.

Then along comes a beautiful, desirable woman offering herself to a vulnerable young man. But Joseph boldly refused. "How . . . could I do such a wicked thing and sin against God?" he told her. He wasn't angry at God for allowing this temptation, but rather trusted in His help and stood firm.

Once we believe God is in control, life becomes more controllable. Mary Bennett's first son, Brian, was born severely brain-damaged because of a physician's error during delivery. Mary said, "I never could have made it through these years of heartache as we've lived with Brian's multiple handicaps if I hadn't believed that God was in charge."

Another woman who was molested by her father from age two until she left home as a teen reflected, "I've come to believe two things that kept me going: God is . . . and God is with us." In the midst of unspeakable pain, the realization that there was a God, and He was with her in the pain kept her spirit alive.

I think Joseph would have shared her perspective. The writer of Genesis said, "The Lord was with Joseph. . . ." No wonder he could relax enough in God's control to become a contributor, even in captivity. And his sense of God's presence provided the accountability he needed to resist the seductive advances of Potiphar's wife.

## Promoted to the Prison

I wanted Joseph's reward for such integrity to be his freedom. I wanted God to guarantee he'd never suffer again. Instead, Potiphar's wife unjustly accused him of rape, and he ended up in prison.

"But while Joseph was there in the prison, the Lord was with him; he showed him kindness and granted him favor in the eyes of the prison warden. So the warden put Joseph in charge of all those held in the prison, and he was made responsible for all that was done there" (Genesis 39:20–22).

Egyptian prisons were dungeons, places of torment and filth. And there was no ACLU, or Chuck Colson, or Chaplain Ray around to comfort the needy or push for prisoner rights.

Had I been Joseph, I would have looked at my prison surroundings and said to God, "Thanks, but no thanks! I don't want favor with the keeper of the prison—I want out!"

But gratitude in the face of adversity is the ultimate expression of faith. The Lord instructs us to welcome suffering as we would a friend (James 1:2–4), and to give thanks in everything that comes our way, be it joyous or pain-provoking (1 Thessalonians 5:18). I believe Joseph must have done this. He didn't give thanks, I'm sure, for the misery of the prison, but for God's miraculous capacity to bring good to him in the most miserable circumstances. And by faith he was content with the good the Lord brought.

Jesus' pain on the cross bought our salvation. Joseph's years of trial honed and positioned him to save the people of God from destruction. What good has come from the suffering you've endured?

On a recent television program, a woman told the story of the death of her grown son. As this grieving mother stood at her boy's open casket, her heart cried out in anger, "God, show me one good thing that could possibly come from this terrible loss."

The answer came at once. Her daughter, who had been estranged from God for years, joined her just then and slipped an arm around her waist. "Mom," the girl said in tears, "my brother's death has touched something deep in me, and I want to come back to the Lord."

Joseph's prison term gave him the chance to serve with his gifts of administration and dream interpretation. He didn't whine about having to use those gifts with no reward but God's pleasure. Instead, Joseph worked with the diligence and skill he would have used had he been serving royalty. And soon, he was!

## From Prison to Palace

Joseph's skill at interpreting dreams got him an overnight promotion to serve as Pharaoh's right-hand man. Once he had the job, his well-developed organizational skills, learned in Potiphar's house and in the prison, allowed him to serve successfully.

During those years of captivity, Joseph was being prepared in his character and his abilities for the destiny he'd dreamed of all his life. Had he resisted God's training program because it didn't happen in the setting he envisioned or come from the trainers he would have chosen, he would have missed his destiny, and the world of his day would have suffered.

We get a glimpse into Joseph's heart when his two sons are born. "Joseph named his firstborn Manasseh and said, 'It is because God has made me forget all my trouble and all my father's household.' The second son he named Ephraim and said, 'It is because God has made me fruitful in the land of my suffering' " (Genesis 41:51, 52).

Joseph's attitude does not negate the impact of his brother's cruelty. Later, when he rejoined his family, the Scripture says Joseph wept, and "his cries were heard all over Egypt." These wrenching sobs came from a heart that knew pain. Even though good came from his brothers' evil actions, their betrayal hurt Joseph deeply. God did not deliver Joseph from heartbreak; he had to live with the memory of what he'd lost, even though good came from it. Joseph rightly felt the pain of loss, but he did not let the pain dictate his response or dull his faith.

Joseph forgave his brothers even before they asked. His heart was at peace about their treatment of him even before they repented. He focused on gratitude for the fruitfulness God had given him in Egypt. In forgiveness he was able to see a sovereign God controlling his life and circumstances.

It would be quite enough for the story to end here. If it had, I think Joseph would have died a contented man. But God blessed Joseph further with the reconciliation of his brothers when his family came to Egypt seeking grain.

The tables had turned completely when his brothers met Joseph at this time. He held all the power, and could have done whatever he wished with them—even had them killed. Instead, he said to them, "Come close to me . . . I am your brother Joseph, the one you sold into Egypt! And now, do not be distressed and do not be angry with yourselves for selling me here, because it was to save lives that God sent me ahead of you

. . . it was not you who sent me here, but God" (Genesis 45:4, 5, 8).

Joseph said no to despair and to temptation; yes to forgiveness and to God's plan. His story makes me long to imitate his faith. I want my confidence in God's leading to enable me to trust Him to bring good from the evil others do to me. I want to forgive as freely and completely as Joseph did, so that I might fulfill the service God ordains for me. I want to trust God as I *wait* for Him to work. It took twenty-two years for Joseph to move from the pit to the palace, not ten minutes. Why shouldn't it take as long for me?

In Matthew 18, Jesus told the story of a wealthy man whose servant owed him the equivalent of $30,000,000. His servant pleaded for mercy, and the gracious master wiped out this monstrous debt.

As the servant went home rejoicing, he saw a man who owed him a mere $17.00. "I want my money *now*," he demanded. When the poor man couldn't pay, the rich man's servant had him thrown into debtor's prison.

When the master heard of his servant's hard-heartedness, he quickly had him sentenced to prison.

The point Jesus was making is this: There are people in our lives who owe us—there is a debt that should be paid. But the debt is only worth $17.00—totally forgivable when we compare it to the $30,000,000 we owe God for how we've wronged Him. Because God has so magnanimously forgiven us, we're beholden to forgive the petty offenses against us.

Trusting in God's sovereignty, we can forgive those who have hurt us. Forgiveness is the secret to keeping our ship moving toward the harbor, icebergs or not.

# 8

# Eliminating Comparison

# Why I Hate the Proverbs 31 Woman

Let's be honest. Haven't you hated the woman Solomon wrote about in Proverbs 31? If I hear once more the extolling of the virtues of this "ideal Christian woman" on Mother's Day, I'm going to scream.

What is my problem? If you don't know, you haven't read Proverbs 31. For the sake of those who have somehow missed it, I will list the characteristics of this paragon of virtue (Is she the woman you'd like to have living on your block . . . or as your mother-in-law?):

- morally perfect
- invaluable
- trustworthy
- inherently good and true
- ingenious
- thrifty
- dutiful
- versatile

- tireless
- joyful
- watchful
- skillful
- charitable
- generous
- fearless
- clever at decorating
- refined in taste
- respected
- industrious
- dependable
- confident
- wise
- kind
- prudent
- energetic
- an ideal wife and mother
- honored by her family
- excelling in virtue
- God-fearing
- deserving
- honored by the public

I suppose she also lifts weights, types 185 words a minute, has a degree in astrophysics, and models for Saks on the side. And her spirituality makes Joan of Arc look like a slouch.

Do you get the sense that I'm slightly intimidated by this woman? Okay, okay. It's true. She makes me nuts because she's all the things I'd love to be, but will never attain. And I hate being reminded of it.

## Will the Real Claire Huxtable Please Stand Up?

Perhaps we all compare ourselves to fantasy figures, even though each generation comes up with its own version of what the perfect woman looks like. For our generation, of course, it's Claire Huxtable, television wife of Bill Cosby. She makes a six-figure salary as a partner in her law firm, yet never brings work home, and rarely seems the least bit stressed by work-related pressures.

Her handsome, athletic, charming husband is an obstetrician, who in six years of episodes has only twice been called away to deliver a baby. Besides running a thriving practice from his home, Dr. Huxtable supervises slumber parties, confers with teachers, cleans the oven, repairs the plumbing, and knows exactly how to comfort the children when the hamster dies. And he never resents his "homebody" status.

With a husband like this, Claire has only to sweep in wearing her $500 suit and sample the spaghetti sauce he's putting together for dinner, then sail out to an evening with her women's book club. She never grocery shops, cleans the toilet, stays up until three in the morning sewing a celery costume for Vegetable Day at school, teaches Bible school, bounces checks, goes to the door without makeup on, or sleeps in a flannel nightie.

Her children never fail in school, wear hand-me-down clothes, burp in public, or complain about having to go to their grandmother's.

If you want discouragement, simply compare your life to hers.

Our mothers' generation had its own version of Claire Huxtable in the now infamous June Cleaver. I was struck by an article by Kay Ebeling in *Newsweek* magazine, which bought into the myth that June Cleaver's fantasy life bore some resemblance to reality. Writing about her growing disillusionment with feminism, Kay Ebeling said, "I'm not advocating that women retrogress to the brainless housewives of the 50's who spent afternoons baking macaroni sculptures and keeping Betty Crocker files. Post-World War II Women were the first to be left with a lot of free time, and they weren't too creative in filling it."

I don't know whom this writer is describing, but I know it isn't my mother. We never saw a macaroni sculpture in our house because my mother was too busy trying to snatch the clothes off the clothesline before the rain came. Meals were cooked without the advantage of mixes and microwaves and deli entrees; the garden was hoed without a tiller. Money stretched tight when the farm simply couldn't produce enough to care for the eight of us.

My mother has lived honorably, but if she had chosen to compare herself with the June Cleaver image, she would have felt like a failure—no pearls, no cloth napkins at dinner, no kids off to Scout camp for the summer.

Such a comparison would have been as evil for her then as it is for us today. Yet we barely even notice that we make comparisons all the time. Just listen to women's conversations. We compare incomes, homes, furniture, husbands, kids, intelligence, status, jobs, bodies, vacations . . . you name it.

Every time I succumb to comparison, I work myself into a tizzy. If the person with whom I rank myself is at all like the Proverbs 31 woman or a neighborhood Claire Huxtable, I wind up on the short end, and become disheartened and disgruntled. If, instead, I come out better than the person I've chosen to compare myself to, I get puffed up and downright revolting. Either way, the Lord isn't pleased.

Paul explained, "We do not dare to classify or compare ourselves with some who commend themselves. When they measure themselves by themselves and compare themselves with themselves, they are not wise" (2 Corinthians 10:12).

## Comparatively Speaking

I'm learning to catch myself more quickly as I move into the comparative mode. Three loaded word-tricks tip me off:

*The "too" trap.* Any time I hear myself say, "I am too fat," or "too talkative" or "too" anything, I know I've gone comparative. What I mean is, "Compared to her, I talk a lot. She's perfect, so if I talk more than she does, I talk too much." Another person has become my standard of perfection, and in that sense, the lord of my life. When we say we're "too" anything, the obvious question arises: by what standard?

*The "-er" error.* Those "-er" suffixes spell comparison every time: bigger, better, taller, smarter, bluer, browner, tanner, healthier, wealthier.

These words always pit me against another, whether it be a real person, or some fantasy figure from a magazine photo. Either way, the "-er" error places me in one corner of a boxing ring, and someone else over in the other corner, where we both wait for the bell to sound so we can come out slugging.

*The "as . . . as" assassination.* We know it when we hear it. "Maybe I spent more than I planned to on this sofa, but at least I didn't spend 'as much as' my sister-in-law. And they don't make nearly 'as much as' we do, either."

One of my personal "I wish I were as pretty as . . ." people is the gorgeous blonde television star Cheryl Ladd. No wonder I listened with such interest when a talk-show host asked her, "If you could, what would you change about yourself?"

Cheryl Ladd looked at him almost incredulously. "My nose, of course," she said. "I'm sure you noticed this hump on it. It's so pronounced, I can only be photographed at limited angles."

I couldn't believe it. Most would consider this woman to represent near physical perfection, yet she thinks she has an unsightly hump on her nose! This woman against whom I'd mentally competed—and lost—had a competition going on in her own head—and she was losing, too.

## The Pharisee Who Compared

Jesus told this story: "Two men went up to the temple to pray, one a Pharisee and the other a tax collector. The Pharisee stood up and prayed about himself: 'God, I thank you that I am not

like other men—robbers, evildoers, adulterers—
or even like this tax collector. I fast twice a week
and give a tenth of all I get.' But the tax collector
stood at a distance. He would not even look up
to heaven, but beat his breast and said, 'God,
have mercy on me, a sinner' " (Luke 18:10–13).

The Pharisee's standard of excellence was
other men; the tax collector's standard was God
himself. The first came away feeling justified,
even though his heart reeked with pride and self-
righteousness. The other man truly was justified,
because he humbled himself and admitted his
sinfulness. It forced him to beg for God's mercy.
At the sweet sound of a sinner's cry for help, Jesus
said, "I tell you that this man, rather than the
other, went home justified before God" (Luke
18:14).

Lately, everywhere we turn, we hear that a
woman's greatest struggle is low self-esteem.
That's why we try all kinds of gimmicks and tech-
niques to shine up our tarnished self-concepts.
We look into the mirror and tell ourselves we're
wonderful. We learn to praise ourselves, stroke
ourselves, and reward ourselves in a desperate
attempt to shore up our sagging self-esteem.

Actually, I'm not sure our problem lies in low
self-esteem at all. The Bible certainly doesn't devote much space to exhorting us on the need for
self-esteem, or instructing us on how to improve
it. But the Scripture does have much to say about
our need to get rid of pride and selfishness.
Could this be our greatest need?

Perhaps when we quit trying to make ourselves as okay as everyone else, repent of the evil

in our hearts, and seek God's mercy, we'll see some change taking place. As we're cleansed by His forgiveness, and warmed by the pleasure in His smile, the self-esteem for which we seek so desperately will quite naturally become ours. We'll know we're significant beings because we're significant to God. Maybe then our comparisons to others will be exposed for what they are.

## Making Peace With the Woman of Proverbs 31

Once I saw the evil of comparing, I began to look at "our lady of perfection" in Proverbs 31 with new eyes. Now I find three things about her that actually *encourage* me.

First, I believe she was an older woman. The Scripture says her children rise up and call her blessed. My children rise up and tell me to fix them breakfast! They don't have the good sense to call me blessed because they haven't yet lived long enough to appreciate all I've done for them.

I had to grow up before I appreciated my mother's sacrifices. For example, every Easter each one of her four daughters had a new dress— different colors, but all matching. I recall her staying up late sewing those dresses. But it wasn't until recently that I realized something even more significant. All those years when we went off to church in those pretty new clothes, Mom never had a new dress. It took becoming a mother myself to realize the sacrifices she made for us. And she made the sacrifice so sweetly, we weren't

even aware it was going on. Now that I'm grown,
I call her blessed.

If the Proverbs 31 woman is older, she's had a
lot of years to mature and develop her wonderful
qualities. Few of us come into qualities like integrity and wisdom and discernment by the time
we're nineteen. But give us another forty or fifty
years of living with Christ, and chances are better
we'll develop many of these traits in our own
lives. Thinking of her as older encourages me to
look to the future with hope, expecting God will
nurture some of these qualities in my own life as
I continue on with Him.

Secondly, I believe this listing of qualities to
be an accounting of her cumulative lifetime accomplishments, rather than a log of a particular
day. If this is true, then following her example
seems much more attainable to me. Perhaps there
were seasons in her life when she spent *most* of
her time managing the household tasks. At another time, she might have given herself to buying fields and growing things, or making belts to
sell to the tradesmen.

The scope of life is long and wide. Opportunities for outside investments simply aren't a pos-
sibility when little ones demand so much of our
energy. Adolescents with their endless soccer
practices and shuttles to the orthodontist require
a different kind of giving. Helping our husband
when he is first coming to be "known in the gates
where they sit among the elders of the land" takes
time, too.

As life goes on, there are seasons when home
and family simply don't demand as much, and

there is more of myself to pour into outer-directed ventures. Over my lifetime, I suspect there will be periods when I make my share of "belts for the tradesmen," and maybe even "plant a vineyard" or two. It's just that I couldn't have done these things at the same time I potty-trained Heidi and helped Steve put together our second music album. One of my desires is to hand-quilt a comforter for each of my children, but this is one desire that will obviously have to wait for a later season of life.

When I look at Proverbs 31 as a lifetime resume, it gives me hope. I don't have to worry when some dreams get pushed aside in the clamor of my family's demands. There'll be a time for them, just as there was for this Israelite woman. God, Solomon reminds us, makes everything beautiful in its time (Ecclesiastes 3:11), and He'll do the same for me and you.

Thirdly, I'm most encouraged when I realize this godliest of all women might well have been Bathsheba. Let me explain. The author of this chapter is King Lemuel. How delighted I was the day I discovered that Solomon was called by six different names, one of which was *Lemuel*. If this Lemuel was indeed Solomon, then the mother who taught him about true womanhood was Bathsheba, a woman whose name has become synonymous with seduction and sin.

It is a tremendous encouragement to think that God's forgiveness is so encompassing that it could take a woman stained with immorality and deception and make her the spokeswoman for feminine godliness.

Perhaps you were pregnant when you got married. Maybe you had the reputation of being "easy." You may come from a family that you find embarrassing. Perhaps you've had an abortion, or borne a child out of wedlock. Remember, it's not where you started that's important. No matter what sin we've committed, we are all bankrupt before God, in desperate need of a Savior. The important thing is that we acknowledge that, ask His forgiveness, and receive His cleansing. Bathsheba received grace, and became the mother of God's anointed king.

And so, I've made peace with this woman of Proverbs 31, now that I'm no longer paralyzed by the evil of comparison. Besides, I see nothing in there about her homemade biscuits. I'll bet they weren't nearly as flaky as mine!

# 9

# Eliminating Competition

# The Contests No One Wins

*Newsweek* magazine labeled it the "Mommy Wars." It's their name for the ugliness generated between females when one group stays home with children, and another group works outside the home, leaving their children in the care of others.

The war rages fiercely. If you don't believe me, watch an episode of "Oprah" when this issue comes up. The friction generated makes Desert Storm look like a Campfire Girls weekend.

And the combatants in this fray go straight for the jugular.

Senator Christopher Dodd of Connecticut told the Senate hearing on child care, "I don't see why we should give a child-care tax credit to women who are at home doing nothing, when we could be supporting women who are out working, making a contribution to society!"[1]

One woman tells of contributing to a panel

---

[1]As quoted in the *Focus on the Family* newsletter, August 1989 edition.

discussion on issues facing the public schools. After the session, another panel member said admiringly, "I was very impressed with your comments. You're so bright that it's hard for me to believe you're just a homemaker." When asked why she didn't slug him, the woman winked and smiled, "I don't believe it's ladylike to flatten people who are so obviously weaker than me."

My work-at-home friends also tire of the phone calls pleading, "We need someone to head up the Brownie troop and be room mother for the third grade and to teach the preschoolers at Bible school. We thought of you since you *don't work* and have *so much time on your hands*." Gr-r-r-r-r.

But the work-away moms get emotional grenades lobbed at them as well.

An older woman in the doctor's waiting room said to a working mother, "Your children certainly seem to be ill a lot. Of course I suppose that's the price you pay when they spend so much time in day care."

A work-at-home mother in the elementary school parking lot said, "How nice you could walk Bobby to school this morning. Otherwise, you'd *never* get to spend time with him, would you?"

The worst attack came from a woman in Sunday morning sharing time: "How thankful I am the Lord helped me see the need to be at home, rather than sacrifice my children to the gods of materialism and self-promotion."

No wonder the battle gets bloody. The wounds go deep, because this is a family feud, sister against sister. Maybe I dislike this animosity so much because I've been on both sides of the fence. When Nathan was a baby, I was a stay-at-home mom while Steve traveled with the singing group, Dogwood. Now I share a career with Steve as an employed mom. I know both the satisfaction and the isolation of being full-time with a little one. And I've experienced both the stimulation and the guilt that comes from an outside career. But what I know best is how much the support of other women means to me as I follow the Lord in whatever path He leads me in. Today, we who should be each others' greatest advocates are becoming archenemies. We're competing, and it's not a pretty sight.

I sometimes see snipping and poking between married and unmarried women, between mothers and women without children, between those with more money and those with less. It's as though we're determined to do battle, and the enemy is any female who's made a different life choice from ours.

## Competition Between Females Isn't a Twentieth-Century Dilemma

We battling women contrast sharply to the women in Scripture who chose to support each other, like Naomi and her daughter-in-law Ruth. Because these two widows chose to care for and support each other, Ruth became the grandmother of King David, and Naomi got a family in her old age. Both women profited.

Mary and Elizabeth each carried a chosen child. But instead of crowing over whose was to be the best, they delighted in elevating the other. As a result, they provided support and sharing neither could have received from anyone else during those fragile and magnificent months as they prepared to be the mother of God's prophet and the mother of God's Son.

But other women in the Bible wanted to scratch each other's eyes out. Rachel and her sister Leah competed continually for the love of their common husband Jacob, as did Sarah and her handmaiden Hagar for the affections of Abraham.

In the Book of First Samuel, Hannah and her husband's other wife Peninnah competed over the issue of children. The Scripture says of Hannah, "Because the Lord had closed her womb, her rival kept provoking her in order to irritate her. This went on year after year. Whenever Hannah went up to the house of the Lord, her rival provoked her till she wept and would not eat" (1 Samuel 1:6, 7). The nastiness we women can display hasn't changed much over the years.

The penchant for competition begins at a young age. In her book *The Friendships of Women*, Dee Brestin tells of the note one little girl wrote to her little friend Ramona. It read:

> *Dear Ramona,*
>> *How are you? I am fine.*
>> *Would you like to be best friends? I like you better than I like Holly. I do not like Holly at all anymore. Let's not like Holly together.*
>> *Your best friend,*
>> *Kate*

One of the most instructive vignettes in Scripture involves the competition between Mary and Martha. Jesus and His disciples had come to rest in the sisters' home. As Jesus relaxed, the two women responded and reacted differently to His presence, each according to their gifts and temperaments.

Mary, it appears, was the more relational and thought of Jesus' emotional needs, so she settled herself at His feet to listen to what He had to share. I know women like Mary—the kind who can sit next to a stack of ironing or a committee report waiting to be written, and turn away from these demands to look me straight in the eye while I tell of my joys and sorrows. Of course, women like this often get so involved with people the ironing *never* gets done, or tomorrow's report invariably comes in two days late.

Martha, on the other hand, was a doer or a server. She saw Jesus' physical needs . . . an attractive meal, a comfortable bed, a place to feel at home in. And she was as right as Mary in her perception of how to care for Him. Working as a team, these two women ministered to the Lord in a complete way, had they been able to see it as such.

But competition reared its ugly head. "Martha," the Bible tells us, "was distracted by all the preparations that had to be made. She came to [Jesus] and asked, 'Lord, don't you care that my sister has left me to do the work by myself? Tell her to help me!' " (Luke 10:40). Martha fairly bristled with self-righteousness and indignation.

God had gifted and called Martha to attend to

the temporal needs of her guests. But at this moment, she served grudgingly. She may have felt put upon, taken advantage of, or jealous of the bond she saw between her sister and Christ. We can hear the resentment in her accusation, "Lord, don't you care. . . ?"

Perhaps at that particular moment, Martha wanted Mary's calling instead of her own because Mary's way of serving Christ appeared less costly. But instead of dealing with her joylessness directly, Martha tried to drag Mary away from the service she was called to render. If Martha was going to be unhappy, at least Mary should be miserable, too!

Instead of criticizing her sister, Martha could have stopped to evaluate herself. Why was she working so feverishly? Had the elaborate dinner plans subtly become a showcase for her culinary skills, rather than a simple service to the Lord? If that were the case, she could have laughed at herself, scrapped the chicken kiev and instead sent out for first-century Israel's version of Kentucky Fried Chicken. No one would have sought her recipe, of course, but her guests would have enjoyed the company of a loving, happy hostess instead of having to squirm under the heaving, guilt-provoking sighs of their overworked benefactor.

Why is it that when we're unhappy we insist on making others around us unhappy, too? Isn't this what we're doing when we pick on our sisters who've made a different choice than ours in the inside/outside work dilemma, or the single/married choice, or the children/no children decision—or the myriad other possibilities that seem to pit us against each other?

## When Other Women Become the Enemy

Sometimes we take potshots at the other side because we're unsure about our own choice.

On the question of staying home with the children, do business women anger you because on some level you resent not being one of them? Or, if you work away from home, do you make snide remarks about at-home moms and their soap-opera addictions because you feel trapped in a too-busy lifestyle, and see no way out?

If you hear yourself taking on single women with guesses about why they haven't been able to "catch a man," could it be that you harbor some jealousy of the freedom they enjoy?

If you're not confident about the life you're living, don't compete or complain. Rather, fight it out with God. That's what Hannah did when her heart was torn over her barrenness. Instead of starting a *Who Needs Mothering, Anyway?* support group, she poured out her heart to God. She made herself open and vulnerable to Him, and in response He answered her prayer and gave her a child.

If you feel stifled and restless at home, ask the Lord if you are living out His plan for you. He could be trying to lead you in another direction, or show you some new arena of service from your home base that you haven't considered. Conversely, if leaving your children at the day care tears you up, go to God about it. Find out if your career plans are His plans for you. If they are, He'll provide for your children's needs. Either way, ask for His guidance and assurance. This challenge holds true any time you sense resentment toward others whose journey has taken a different turn from yours.

There could be other reasons why you feel other women are your enemies. Maybe you believe God has called you to your present circumstances, and you love the up-side of what He's given you to do. But you weren't prepared for the cost of this calling, and now that it's beginning to demand more of you, you feel resentment.

Working at home can be isolating. It often lacks the stimulation of a job outside. It's generally an unrespected profession, so women at home can easily feel devalued. And there's no paycheck, so you may live with financial struggles that never seem to ease.

But working outside the home has its own cost. Never, never will you feel like you have enough time for everything. You will face having less time with your children, and the sadness or guilt of not being able to contribute as much to school, church, scouting, and other volunteer activities.

Singleness has its freedom, but it's also lonely. Marriage gives security and companionship, but limits your life options because you must consider your partner.

Every choice has its consequences—some pleasant, others not so pleasant. Jesus reigns as the Savior of the world, but the price of His position was His death on the cross.

Maybe you've never squarely faced the consequences of your life choices, deciding to embrace the price as well as the pleasure.

When we're competitive with others, it often means we either aren't sure of our own calling, or we don't like what it's costing us. Either way, we need to abandon competition and relocate the field of battle to our own hearts, where it belongs.

## The Alternative to Competition

Instead of competing, begin to change by *reinforcing the choices you've made.*

If you're an at-home mom, join a mother's support group at your church, or subscribe to the *Welcome Home* newsletter, a publication especially designed for the unique needs of a mother at home. Make friends of other work-at-home mothers so you can trade babysitting or garage sale together or picnic at the park and talk grown-up books while the kids demolish the sandbox.

If you work away from home, schedule a luncheon fellowship for women like yourself, and share ideas on getting the family to help with housework, or pray with each other about the man in the next office who takes credit for your ideas.

If you're unmarried, join up with a group of bright, aggressive singles who see the potential for joy and service in the life you live. Also, pick your married friends from those who see you as a vital contributor to life, rather than a sorry excuse for an "unclaimed blessing." Likewise, married women should choose friends who support married life. I shuddered when I overheard a hairdresser say that even though she's married, every Friday night she goes out with her single girlfriends. It was clear from the conversation that her friends see marriage as a trap, not a joy. I wonder to myself what kind of support this young wife will experience when she and her husband go through their next misunderstanding. Will these friends encourage her to work it through, or to nurse hurt feelings?

Whatever you've chosen for your life needs to be respected and valued by the people closest to you.

Also, *enjoy the benefits* of your choice. Work-at-home moms often have more flexibility to plan personal development. You can take a class that interests you, even if it doesn't contribute to a degree. You're home to be with the kids, so be with them. Play dolls for an hour if it strikes your fancy, and don't worry so much about what looks "productive." These are the pleasures of the life you've chosen.

If yours is an away-from-home job, you likely have lots of stimulation, so enjoy it! Give your spare time in conversation and friendship to those the Lord has given you at the workplace without always harboring nagging guilt about not being with your kids. If God has led you to spend these hours apart from your family, He'll care for them. You may have more money at your disposal than your work-at-home sister, so a cleaning person may not be a necessary luxury for you. Use your money to buy yourself and your family time together.

Finally, *connect to your counterpart*. If you work at home, make a friend who works away. If you are married, get close to single women. If you're childless, spend time with families who have children. If your kids are teens, take on some family babysitting ventures for a couple with preschoolers. Venturing outside our little world will help us recall the similarities between us, rather than always focusing on the differences.

God intends that we complement, not compete. Let's lay down our arms and end the "Mommy Wars" and the "Marriage Wars" and the "Money Wars" and any other conflicts that divide us as sisters in Christ. We need each other, and the Lord will use us as well to take the good news of His peace to all the other sisters-to-be who don't know of His love.

# 10

## Establishing Acceptance

# Lifting Just One Finger for God

The old Russian woman lay on the sofa, propped by pillows to keep her from toppling over. Multiple sclerosis had twisted her body almost beyond recognition.

Corrie ten Boom had come to visit her that night, using the cover of darkness to escape detection by the Lithuanian authorities. When Corrie walked across the room and kissed the woman's wrinkled cheek, she could respond only by rolling her eyes and smiling because the atrophied muscles in her neck would no longer allow her to move her head. The only part of her body she could still control was her right hand, and with her gnarled knuckles she stroked Corrie's face. Corrie reached up to take her hand, and kissed the index finger. With little more to use than an index finger, this brave woman served God.

Every morning the woman's husband would

prop her into a sitting position on the sofa, and place their battered typewriter on a little table in front of her. The old woman would begin to type. Using one finger to peck out the letters, she would translate Christian books into Russian. She typed portions of the Bible and the books of Billy Graham, Watchman Nee, and others.

For the ministry she'd been given, the old woman saw her sickness as a prerequisite, not a detriment. Every other Christian in the city was watched by the secret police. But because she had been sick so long, the police took no interest in this woman, and she could work undetected.

"Not only does she translate these books," her husband told Corrie, "but she prays while she types. Sometimes it takes a long time for her finger to hit the key, or for her to get the paper in the machine, but all the time she is praying for those whose books she is working on."[1]

Life puts limitations on us; no one is without them. But once we accept those limitations, God is free to use us in our weakness to glorify himself.

Now, I have some good news and some bad news about our limitations. First the bad news.

### Bad News #1: You Can't Have It All.

During the seventies, some foolish crusaders took to the airwaves, magazine pages, and conference circuits, announcing women could at last have it all. Sizzling marriage, precocious children,

---

[1]As told in *Tramp for the Lord*, Corrie ten Boom with Jamie Buckingham, (Jove Books, 1976).

skyrocketing career—we were going to have it all, all at once. Bring home the bacon, fry it up in a pan, never let him forget he's a man . . . and correct eleven pages of math homework in between.

In the eighties we discovered we didn't *have* it all; we were simply having to *do it all.* And it wasn't nearly as much fun as the television commercials made it out to be. One woman said, "I'm exhausted all the time. Right now I'm the only person in the office who could be called a Superwoman, and most of the people I work with don't know how I do it. I don't know how I do it, either, but I don't have a choice about it. Much of my life seems to go by in a blur."

I forgot to put bacon on the shopping list. No time to fry it, anyway, with a zoning committee meeting at 7:00. The man? Around here somewhere, I think, but hoping I won't notice him because he knows I know it was his turn to clean the bathrooms and he went golfing after work instead.

## Bad News #2: You Can't Be in Two Places at the Same Time.

If you're hooked on *I Love Lucy* reruns, and the *MacNeil-Lehrer Report* airs at the same time, you can't watch both on my TV, no matter how much you'd like to be both escapist and educated. Life demands choices, and choices have consequences.

When Steve and I agree to a year-long concert schedule, we're also choosing not to be as vitally involved in our church as we'd like, because we're gone nearly every weekend. We do attend a Tuesday morning service our church provides for weekend travelers like us, but it isn't the same. There's no Sunday school, no choir. That's a choice I don't like having to make, but we can't be doing a concert and attending our own worship service in the same Sunday time slot.

Living in Nashville means we're close to the hub of the music industry, but we're also eight hours away from our beloved parents. Now that they're older, helping them requires more time on the road between our house and theirs every year. But those hours of driving are the price we must pay, because we can't live in two places at once.

## Bad News #3: You Have Only 24 Hours In a Day—and You Have to Sleep During Some of Them.

Our bodies have limits, no matter how determined we are. We can go only so long without sleep, absorb so much information, make so many decisions, and do well at so many things. Human beings were designed with limitations. If you're not as yet convinced, just wait until you turn forty!

All this bad news boils down to one thing: life has limits. The sooner we start acting like limited creatures and quit trying to be God, the sooner God can begin to help us.

## When Others Don't Accept Our Limits

One woman said to me, "I make all my decisions out of fear." Sometimes the fear of missing out controls her. Other times she fears getting left behind. Most often, however, she fears displeasing the people around her. When we live to please others, we're letting them set the limits on our lives.

Jesus pleased only one person, His Father. The Pharisees weren't pleased with Him. The crowds turned on Him. Even His closest disciples didn't always rave about His decisions. But He played His life to an audience of one, and could therefore disappoint others, yet have His heart at rest.

Bill Cosby once said, "I don't know the secret to success, but I know the key to failure—it's trying to please everyone."

Often the limits others choose for us aren't the same ones God has chosen, so we have to say no to others' requests.

Joan Sturkie is a working mother of eight children, so she knows firsthand what it means to be pulled in a thousand directions at once. If she let others set the limits for her life with their requests, she'd never know peace. So she found ways to simplify decisions. In her book *Enjoy Your Kids, Enjoy Your Work* she offers sound advice on how to choose a response when you've just been asked for the umpteenth time to serve on a committee, or come to a Tupperware party, or be the one in the office who learns the new software first. She has these suggestions:

- *Take time before answering.* Stand firm, even if you're being pressured to give an answer immediately.
- *Evaluate how badly you are really needed.* I often ask myself, "Is this a job someone else could do as well as I could?" If it is, I may be stealing someone else's opportunity to serve the Lord by saying yes.
- *Ask yourself what your motives are for taking the job.* Are you flattered at being asked? Are you responding simply out of guilt or duty? Maybe God isn't helping in the tasks we've taken on because we've chosen them to promote ourselves, improve our image, free ourselves from false guilt, or impress someone else. Why should He help us if what we're doing is meant to promote ourselves rather than His kingdom?
- *Look at your present time schedule and see if it will be possible to add anything else.*
- *Question how it will affect your family.* If it means giving up family time, talk to them before eliminating that time.
- *Pray about your decision.*
- *Make a decision and stand by it.* Don't give in to pressure to change your mind, even if the caller whines, or you have second thoughts.
- *Be joyful in your decision.* If new information comes to light later that indicates you might have made the wrong choice, don't look back. You can learn from your mistake. And rest assured that if doing the task really had been crucial, God would have made that abundantly clear. If He didn't, realize that even if you make a different choice at

the next opportunity, this time what you did was fine.

Not being controlled by the passion to please everyone will free you to make better decisions. For instance, when your third grader's teacher calls requesting cookies for the Valentine party, you'll be free to ask yourself, "Which do I have more of, time or money?" If the answer is time, you may wind up baking those wonderful decorated hearts all the kids will squeal about. But if time is short, you'll be free to let the bakery do the baking, or else elect to send a package of Double-Stuff Oreos—the hands-down choice over home-baked cookies every time among the kids I know.

Steve's Grandma, Maude Steele, is my model of a woman with courage in her convictions. If Grandma Steele didn't want to accept an invitation to go somewhere, she'd just say, "No." If the person inviting her asked why, she'd respond, "I don't want to." There were no excuses about having a headache, or one of the babies feeling poorly. If Grandma Steele didn't want to go, she said no. I do admire the way she knew her mind, and spoke it, even if she might offend others.

Her example helped me on my last doctor's visit. My most dreaded experience in the examination room isn't putting on the paper dress; it's the nurse saying, "You can get on the scales now."

I detest being weighed by someone else. I feel stripped and guilty and vulnerable, exposing my poundage to a total stranger. So on my last appointment, when the nurse indicated it was weigh-in time, I said, "No." I did. And it felt great! I did explain I'd gained about three pounds since my visit a year ago, but I refused to be weighed. I declined without excuses, explanations, or apologies. The nurse wasn't offended. How chagrined I was to realize I'd spent so many years postponing, then dreading, these physicals because I so hated being weighed. I should have said no years before! Learning to take a chance on being displeasing is one of the more liberating lessons I've learned recently. It's given me a new joy in my decisions, and I believe the Lord is pleased.

Because we do have limits, we need to be determined not to let others push us to operate outside our God-given limitations. But there's good news, too.

## The Good News: Saying Yes to Our Limits Unlimits God!

We may be spending far too much energy in life running from our limitations. For example, you may think you're unusable to God because you struggle with emotional pain, but you are wrong.

The famous preacher Charles Spurgeon was frequently confined to bed for weeks at a time by psychological and physical illness. Prolonged bouts of depression often plagued him. Yet he published over 3,500 sermons and wrote 135 books. Many regarded him as the outstanding preacher of his generation.

Spurgeon was able to achieve such accomplishments in spite of his depression because he came to see his problems as part of God's work in his life. He allowed them to make him more sensitive to others in pain. Eventually he observed that an unusual spiritual blessing often followed periods of great psychological suffering, so he began to see the depression as a herald of a new work that God was beginning, instead of as an enemy.

Spurgeon's solution makes me think of the apostle Paul and his struggle with what he described only as his "thorn in the flesh." Some feel it was a physical ailment that was not only painful, but also disfiguring. I get the feeling Paul hated it, because he reports that three times he "pleaded" with the Lord to take it away. If you read the New Testament, you'll see that the strident Paul wasn't one to plead with anyone about much of anything. He might issue orders, but he rarely pleaded. Yet in this case, he describes his action with a word that indicates a sense of near-desperation. He wanted deliverance from this limitation in his life.

With his limitation he did two things we can do as well.

First, he insisted on God's perspective. Paul asked for God's help, and seemed unwilling to let God off the hook until He responded. The Lord answered with words that brought Paul peace.

Paul reported, "He said to me, 'My grace is sufficient for you, for my power is made perfect in weakness' " (2 Corinthians 12:9). Paul wasn't willing to settle for a secondhand answer.

Though he may have conferred with others, or sought others' prayers, the answer that satisfied his soul came straight from God. He seemed insistent on keeping after God until the answer came.

Have you confronted God about your limits, or are you trying to buy into the answers He's given others? God loves to be pursued. Hannah confronted God about her barrenness, and made such a fuss the priest assumed she was drunk. I admire a woman who will do battle with God like Hannah did. Her husband had taken his best shot at answering her pain: "Don't I mean more to you than ten sons?" But Hannah wanted to hear God's voice for herself. He responded, and she came away with a heart at peace.

God's voice does that, and it did for Paul, too. God told Paul to expect His power in greater measure, and in that promise, Paul found rest.

Secondly, Paul chose a faith response to his limits and stuck to it. After God explained the grace Paul could access, Paul accepted His words. "Therefore," he said, "I will boast all the more gladly about my weaknesses, so that Christ's power may rest on me. That is why, for Christ's sake, I delight in weaknesses, in insults, in hardships, in persecutions, in difficulties. For when I am weak, then I am strong" (2 Corinthians 12:9, 10).

Paul let go. He stopped struggling to be freed of his limitation. Instead, he focused his energy on joy. He let the weakness that had discouraged him become a catalyst for praise and expectancy. Instead of a stumbling block to fulfillment, it became a stepping stone to greater usefulness.

Admirable women of the faith all had limits. Catherine Booth was sickly. Susanna Wesley was hounded by a lifetime of poverty. Harriet Tubman was unattractive and illiterate. Florence Nightingale was a woman trying to make it in an exclusively man's world.

But these limitations didn't limit God at all. They only served to make it clearer that the work these women accomplished was by His power and grace alone. Greater glory, not less, came to Him because of their limitations.

My favorite example of someone whose limits didn't limit God is Helen Keller. Although blind and deaf, she graduated *cum laude* from Radcliffe, authored seven books and countless articles, traveled the continent educating people about the needs of the handicapped, toured in vaudeville, and made a silent movie.

A poem she wrote reveals how she saw her own limitations. She looked to others with limits for her own courage and strength. Milton's blindness and Beethoven's deaf ears didn't keep them from being able to give; with God's help, her handicaps didn't need to limit her, either. Helen Keller wrote:

> They took away what should have been my eyes.
> (But I remembered Milton's *Paradise*.)
> They took away what should have been my ears.
> (Beethoven came and wiped away my tears.)
> They took away what should have been my tongue.

(But I had talked with God when I was young.)
He would not let them take away my soul.
(Possessing that I still possess the whole.)

## Sometimes Acceptance Comes Only After We Say "Uncle"

Annie Chapman is the original homing pigeon; traveling has never been my game. I like my own house, my own bed, my own cooking. In addition, I never wanted to be a professional singer. I like to sing, but I never had the passion to sing for a living. The stage has never held allure for me.

That's why years ago when Steve proposed I join him in a traveling singing ministry, I flatly refused.

He'd been touring with Dogwood, but we both could see how his absence was tearing up our family. Nathan learned to count to twenty-one as he kept track of how many days Daddy was going to be gone each time he left. Steve once reprimanded him, and two-and-a-half year old Nathan shot back, "Old Man, why don't you get in that motor home and take another trip?"

Something had to change or we'd have no family left, but the change I wasn't willing to make was to travel with Steve. I wanted to be at home. I also felt that the road was no place to raise children. Being with others all the time, no privacy, no stability—what kind of life was this to offer to children?

As I struggled with the decision, I began to

have a recurring dream that I was unfaithful to Steve. Steve is the only man I've ever even kissed, so naturally these dreams shook me terribly. What could they mean? Was God trying to show me a bent in my heart to immorality that I wasn't aware of?

As I prayed, the answer came. I was being unfaithful to Steve, not by sexual sin but by forcing him to abandon God's call on his life to minister with music. Finally I saw the issue as one of obedience to God. Although I was sure I didn't have what it took to raise a family on the road, and I knew my own insecurity as a performer, God was asking me to submit to His will. Finally the choice was clear. I'd give in to the Lord, or I'd live outside His call. There would be no in-between.

So I said yes. My submission brought peace, but it didn't make life comfortable. For most of the years that have followed, I've never felt "at home" on the road. I have learned, though, that home can be wherever our family is together, if I let God help us. Also, I've seen the Lord give us *more* time together as a family, not less, because we've traveled all these years. We are friends as well as family. The children have blossomed, too, even though I expected they would wither. Heidi is naturally shy, but these years of being with people have developed her confidence, and now she wants to use her gift of music publicly.

What is God asking of you? What are your limits? Have you accepted them? Are you willing to let God make use of your right index finger, if that's all you have to give? Come join the company where most of us are too old, too tired, too sick, too poor, too insecure, or too plain to do very much for God. Then we'll see what God can do to create extraordinary works from such ordinary specimens.

# 11

# Establishing Endurance

# Finishing the Race With Your Torch Still Lit

In the Greek games, marathon runners raced against each other for the coveted victory wreath. In these games, however, one thing was different from modern marathons. Each runner held aloft a lighted torch. The winner of the race was the one who came in first—with his torch still lit.

I can't imagine a better picture of the race of life. Winning isn't simply a matter of coming in first; it depends as much on finishing the run with the light inside us still burning bright. That light is a gentle and quiet spirit, full of peace and hope, which stays alive even when darkness closes in all about us.

Keeping the torch lit often requires running more slowly than you would if finishing was your only concern. It can also mean stopping along the way if rain pelts down, or getting help if your fuel supply gets low. It may call for taking a more circuitous route if the wind along the main highway blows fiercely enough to threaten the flame. Whatever it takes, God wants us to cross the finish line with our torches still burning bright.

## Slowing the Race so Your Torch Won't Go Out

Last year our whole family took a popular personality test. Steve's results came out just as I expected: his profile described him as steady and compliant. Mine, however, was summed in one ugly word: driven. A friend who saw my results said later, "This means you're not much fun to live with, but you can sure get the work done!"

I was not born to be patient. I like to eat fast, talk fast, go fast, think fast. If I keep this up, Steve tells me, I'm going to die fast. So I'm learning to slow my pace.

I've found excellent help in thoughts from Jo Coudert, a writer from *Woman's Day* magazine. She suggests five ways to slow the race.

1. *Slow down by allowing a margin for error.* We impatient people don't like to waste time, so we're always cutting things too close. If I think an afternoon can comfortably accommodate four errands, I plan six. Then when a child's tardiness throws me off schedule, I have no flexibility, and I pop my cork. Had I simply planned three tasks, with a fourth on the list if it worked out, unexpected delays could have been taken in stride.

If there's something for which I absolutely have to be on time, like an airline departure, or a concert opening, I relax more if I allow ridiculous amounts of time. Then if a tire goes flat, or Nathan loses the belt to his britches, I have time to manage the crisis without coming unglued.

2. *Slow down by asking, "Is this worth my peace?"* The light of God's peace stays shining if I don't give in to fears and regrets. If we're screaming off to a movie, only to have to go back home because Heidi forgot to turn the iron off, I've been known to go berserk. But that's when I need to ask myself, "Is this worth giving up my peace?" Maybe we'll miss the first ten minutes of the movie, but it won't mean the end of Western civilization.

Life goes on. Maybe getting to the mall after closing time means I don't get my new Keds at 35% off, but is saving a few dollars worth dimming the light inside? God provides all our resources anyway; He can provide the extra for the Keds if He chooses not to supply through the sale.

3. *Slow down by planning for the worst.* Impatience hits when life seems to be thwarting my time table. Now I try to see these slow-ups as little rest stops along the highway of life. It helps to keep a notepad in my purse so I can jot down things to do while I wait in a grocery line. Or I grab the minutes to hit the headlines of the *National Inquirer,* just in case an Elvis sighting has taken place in the near vicinity and I should be informed. Smile.

Airports seem to swallow up vast amounts of our time during flight delays and weather hold-ups. I've learned to plan for the wait. When the kids were smaller, and we were traveling by van,

I'd carefully plan to pack the special books and toys so they'd be sure to have favorites along. Once during a 21-day, 4,000-mile trip across Texas and Arizona without air-conditioning in the company of two children, ages five and two, we splurged on a small TV that would play through the 12-volt system of the van. Later we added a VCR. Bible story videos, a few Disney films, and *Little House on the Prairie* episodes kept all of us from insanity. Cassette players—*with headphones*—helped too. (Take it from me. Even a Christian artist like Amy Grant loses her appeal after the 34th time. I suspect now that Amy has children, she'd be quick to agree.)

We also provided a goodie bag with prizes for special accomplishments, like memorizing a Bible verse, finishing a book, or reciting a poem.

Now that Nathan and Heidi are older, they plan for the worst themselves. They've learned to pack their own music tapes and books. If we're driving, they sometimes bring a friend along. On trips that we know are going to be particularly grueling, the kids occasionally opt to stay with Grandma and Grandpa.

4. *Slow down by making joy for someone else.* When I'm impatient, I usually make others around me miserable. But rarely do I suffer alone. If I'm stuck in a slow check-out line, others behind me are, too. If I can concentrate on making it a bit easier for them, I fare better. It doesn't take much—a smile perhaps, or a bit of light conversation—but it pulls my focus off me, and helps me get hold of peace.

I've even tried to use these check-out holdups to work on growing in Christian virtue. Sometimes if the person behind me has only a few items, I invite them to go ahead of me. Unfortunately, I've expected God would reward me by having the favor returned. But the last time I had to pay for only three items, I got stuck behind three carts crammed with stuff, and nobody made a move to let me go ahead. *God,* I found myself complaining, *I was so generous last week, now no one is being generous to me.* Then it came to me. My little act of kindness the week before didn't teach me much about faithfulness. I was the magnanimous giver then, and the giving cost me little. But to give these people in line a smile and a gracious word when I instead wanted to run them down and push to the front of the line—that would be an act of generosity.

Becoming a giver helps me keep control when everything around me seems out of control. Could this be why the Scripture says it's more blessed to give than to receive?

5. *Slow down by giving up self-importance.* Impatience says, "I am the queen of the world. I deserve what I want, when I want it. And I want it *now.* Everyone else should stand aside because my life is the most important one here, and my wants deserve to come first."

But we're servants of Christ, not masters of others. It's our pleasure to live life at the Master's bidding, and on His grand, eternal timetable. Sometimes His timing moves faster than ours, at other times, more slowly. Either way, our call is to submit to His timing and relax in His care.

## Knowing Enough to Come in From the Rain

Running too fast can put out our light, but the rain of troubles can drown it. We've got to see what troubles are avoidable, or the light won't last. God's peace can weather the fiercest storm. In fact, that's what sets His peace apart from the calm the world offers. His peace holds steady in the midst of pain, not just in the absence of pain.

However, some of the pain we feel in life isn't God-inflicted, or even life-inflicted; it's self-inflicted. God doesn't promise to bless us when we insist on operating outside the natural parameters He shows us in life. He doesn't promise to keep our torch lit if we insist on running in the rain.

To live within the boundaries of the physical, emotional, and financial limitations we've been given isn't faithlessness; it's submission born of true wisdom.

Living within His parameters means we don't take on every fight that comes along, even if it's a fight for right. Have you ever thought of all the things Jesus did *not* do when He was on earth? God's people lived as political slaves to the evil Romans, yet Jesus didn't start a movement to free them. Hunger and poverty abounded in the world, and Jesus twice miraculously fed multitudes, but He didn't organize an ongoing soup kitchen, or build a YMCA that could take in the homeless. There are hundreds of legitimate causes He could have championed. And He had power to make genuine changes. Even though He didn't, He still ended His earthly years claiming, "I have brought you glory by completing the work you gave me to do" (John 17:4).

If Jesus could live and die without directly serving every worthy cause, and still finish His life with a sense of completion, then surely we can, too.

The guidance counselor at Nathan's school has this sign posted in her office:

> Do not feel
> totally
> personally
> irrevocably
> responsible
> for everything.
> That's my job.
> Love,
> God

## Continuing to Run When You're Finishing Last

When Abraham Lincoln was a young man, he was badly swamped in an attempt to be elected to the state legislature. Next he entered business. He failed dismally, and spent the next seventeen years of his life paying off the debts of a worthless partner.

Next he was badly defeated in a race for Congress. He failed to get a sought-after appointment to the U.S. Land Office. In a race for the U.S. Senate, he lost by a wide margin. He then ran for the Vice-Presidency and lost. In 1858, Douglas defeated him in the presidential contest.

Eventually he won, of course, and went on to be one of our greatest presidents—not in spite of his failures, but because he endured them and got up to try again.

Staying in the race when it looks like it's all uphill takes endurance. However, endurance, like biceps, can be developed.

*Connect to God's Word.* Reading the Scriptures and praying can help us develop endurance. Get involved in a Bible study with women who are going through the same struggles you are. God didn't intend this be a solo journey. Although it doesn't always appear to be, life truly is a team sport. Even God the Father draws from the Son and the Holy Spirit. For us to act independently sets us up as more spiritual than He. Much of what He gives us of His life—courage—and per-spective—comes to us through His people. We need to be connected to them so His life has a channel through which it can flow to us.

*Care for your mind.* Read biographies of strong women from the past or enjoy some excellent novels. Listen to good music. Tape your favorite radio show so you can hear it later undistracted. And *turn off the mindless TV!* Television can be a most stimulating friend, but it can also be a se-ductive enemy that saps your resolve and under-mines your courage.

*Be kind to your heart.* Make the effort to have lunch with a friend you simply enjoy. Don't begrudge yourself the time it takes daily to keep a journal. You'll stay in touch with your private thoughts, and have a better barometer reading of the condition of your inner life.

*Look for ways to laugh.* Life is tragic, but it is also immeasurably funny. Humor is a great distancer, and can keep you from taking too seriously what God refuses to.

A few months ago, an older woman approached me after a concert and said, "Oh, Annie. From way up in the balcony where I was sitting, you looked so young and pretty. Now that I'm up close, though, I can see you're neither one."

I was taken aback, of course, and choked out, "That's an interesting observation."

Apparently my response was not good enough. She wanted me to not only know I wasn't a beauty, but also to appreciate her bringing it to my attention. She repeated her statement over again.

This time I decided to give her what she wanted. "Thank you," I said smiling. At that she turned away, apparently satisfied.

When I told Steve about the encounter, he laughed so hard we nearly had to carry him out of the room. The original comment wasn't particularly funny, but the woman's insistence that I must thank her for her unkindness struck us both as hilarious.

Besides looking for the humor in life, we're learning to value those who help us laugh. We have dear friends who make the zaniest home videos you can imagine. For these home-produced sitcoms they do costumes, props, the works. The Normans know how to laugh at life, and they help us do the same.

Laughter helps keep the torch lit while we run the race of life, and that's our goal, after all.

If we can learn to run more slowly, seek shelter when it's raining, and keep on even though we may be finishing last, we'll cross the finish line and come face-to-face with the welcoming smile of the Lord.

# 12

# Establishing Vision

# Changing the World With a Wooden Spoon

What would it take to change the world? An army of millions? Billions of dollars? The mind of a genius? Political power?

These questions erupted in Moses' mind after the Lord met him in the burning bush. "Go change Egypt," God had commanded him. Moses responded exactly as I would have. He looked up, incredulous, and stammered, *"How?"*

Moses knew well the impossibility of the task. He grew up in Pharaoh's court, knew firsthand the sophistication and arrogance of Egypt's ruling class. Historians believe Ramses II had taken the throne of Egypt during Moses' years in exile, and Egypt under Ramses was at its economic and political apex. Builders crafted extraordinary architecture; art forms flourished; trade burgeoned. And one sheepherder from the backside of the desert with orders was supposed to march in and take control? No wonder Moses was astounded!

"Lord," Moses pleaded, "what if they do not believe me or listen to me?"

God said to him, "What is that in your hand?"

Moses held a simple shepherd's staff, the basic everyday tool of his trade, just as a plumber would hold a wrench, or an accountant a calculator. But Moses knew he couldn't change the world with a shepherd's staff.

"Throw it on the ground," the Lord told him.

As soon as he did, the staff became a snake. Moses ran from it.

"Pick it up by the tail," God instructed.

Trembling, Moses reached out for the snake. When he grabbed onto its tail, it stiffened and became his familiar staff again.

After that, the staff is called "the staff of God" in Scripture, and it becomes a holy tool in Moses' hand to change the course of world history.

## What Is That in Your Hand?

With a mandate to free the three million people of Israel from slavery in Egypt, the terrified Moses surely searched furtively for the massive, flashy, prestigious resources any fool could see would be needed to get the job done. But God simply told him to look at what he had in his hand.

God knew what Moses held in his hand; the question was asked for Moses' benefit. The sheepherder wouldn't have thought his staff to be the only weapon he'd need for victory, because he didn't know how much God could do with ordinary things when they are made available to Him.

What do you have in your hand? A wooden spoon? That spoon could turn out a cake or a pie that would show God's love to your neighbor. The pen you hold could produce a note of encouragement to your teenager who struggles in the next room. The Dr. Seuss book on your lap could make a moment with your child say, "Yes, I'm busy, but I'm never too busy for you." Your hairbrush could send the message to your husband, "You are worth the effort it takes to look wonderful for you."

What's that in your hand? A telephone? It could be the vehicle to help a new divorcee face the pain of being alone today, or to allay the fears of a new mother who doesn't know how to cope with her baby's crying.

Is there money in your hand? It could buy a baby quilt for the Crisis Pregnancy Center, or a bag of groceries for the family whose husband and father lost his job.

Sometimes we try too hard to assemble and polish the perfect tools to serve God. He doesn't need better tools. He's well-equipped to accomplish what needs to be done. And because the battles we face are spiritual, not temporal, the abilities and talents we add to our arsenal aren't necessarily the ones needed. What God desires is that we trust Him, and give Him what we already hold in our hands.

## Six Women Who Opened Their Hands

*Jael, staking a claim for God.* You may not have heard of Jael, the wife of Heber. Queen of Nothing, Mrs. No-one-special. But this brave woman felled a military commander without a sword or spear or javelin. She trusted God and used what was in her hand.

Israel had gone to battle against the armies of Canaan. Although the people of God defeated Canaan, the commander of the Canaanite troops, Sisera, escaped. Unless he was killed, he'd certainly muster another army, and Israel would still be in danger.

Sisera ran toward Jael's tent for refuge. Jael cleverly invited him in, and offered to hide him from his pursuers. Exhausted from the battle, he asked for a drink of water. Jael gave him warm milk instead, (what better way to induce sleep?) covered him, and waited until he'd fallen into a deep slumber.

Then she took a tent peg and hammer, tiptoed over to the sleeping man, and drove the peg through his temple and into the ground!

Her act of courage marked the turning point for Israel. The Scripture says, "On that day God subdued Jabin, the Canaanite king, before the Israelites. And the hand of the Israelites grew stronger and stronger against Jabin, the Canaanite king, until they destroyed him" (Judges 4:23, 24).

Jael could have wasted much of her life preparing for this moment by leaving her family and going off to learn how to sling a spear, or getting an ulcer trying to work her way up through the ranks of the military. Had she done these things, she might have missed developing the only skills she really needed, the mother's sense to give warm milk so he'd sleep deeply, and a nomadic wife's ability to wield a tent-planting hammer. The fact that she lacked military skills only made the victory more obviously God's, and He received glory He might not have received had a skillful soldier taken Sisera's life instead.

Jael's mission makes me think of the Amy Grant song that says, "All I ever have to be is what You made me."[1] If we're faithful, and full of faith, what He makes of us will be more than enough to accomplish all He intends for us to do.

*Abigail, the gracious gourmet.* Abigail ranks equally high on my list of Bible women who used what was in their hand.

When David was on the run from King Saul (1 Samuel 25), he offered protection to the herdsmen of Nabal. But instead of rewarding David, Nabal treated him contemptuously, and David vowed revenge.

When the news of David's impending attack reached Abigail, Nabal's wife, she knew all would be lost unless she acted. So she gathered the food she had on hand: two hundred loaves of bread, two skins of wine, five dressed sheep, five bushels of roasted grain, a hundred cakes of raisins, and two hundred cakes of pressed figs, and went to meet David.

When she found him, she bowed at his feet, deftly apologized, and appealed to his chivalry until David's anger abated. In so doing, Abigail not only saved her household, but protected God's anointed from having to live with the guilt of a senseless slaughter. David was saved from

---

[1] From the song *All I Ever Have to Be.*

carrying out his revenge through the brave and timely action of Abigail.

She didn't lament her lack of weaponry when faced with the challenge of stopping an invading army, she simply used what she had available.

*Dorcas, keeping them in stitches.* We know little about Dorcas, except that she lived in Joppa and spent her life doing good and helping the poor. Her most dramatic moment came after her death.

At her wake, those she had loved showed the apostle Peter the beautiful clothes she had crafted for them. He understood her ministry to be so essential that he asked the Lord to restore her life, and she was raised from the dead! (Acts 9:36–42).

If we had to list kingdom gifts we couldn't do without, we probably wouldn't rate sewing in the top ten. Preaching, perhaps, or Bible teaching, street witnessing, or serving on the foreign field. Crafting clothing wouldn't be on a list of world-changing ventures, to our way of thinking, but God must not agree. We have no scriptural record of a preacher, Bible teacher, or singer rendering service so essential to the kingdom they couldn't be allowed to leave the earth. But Dorcas was brought back from the dead . . . to sew. That simple skill, mixed with love and used with faithfulness, made her life irreplaceable.

*Rose Totino, power with a pizza paddle.* When God asked Rose Totino, "What's that in your hand?" the answer may have been "Pepperoni with extra thick crust." That answer was more than good enough for God to be able to mold a world-changer.

Rose and her husband Jim founded the famed

Totino's Pizza Company in a small bakery in Minneapolis. When they decided to make the risky move to frozen pizza, the company nearly folded. In the days of desperation that followed their near-foreclosure, Rose became open to the gospel message and gave her heart to Christ.

In the years ahead, God didn't call Rose to board up the bakery and move to the African jungles. He simply asked her to take the skills in her hand, and the money and prestige she gained from the business, and use her gifts to further His cause. And so she has, by contributing generously to Christian organizations, and speaking about Christ to people around the world.

*Grandma Moses, genius with a brush.* Grandma Moses wasn't on any professional track to become a major force in the world of American art. She didn't sell her first painting until she was a 78-year-old widow, and that one sold quite by accident. Art dealer Louis Caldor stopped for lunch at a drugstore in the tiny village of Hoosick Falls, New York. As he walked in, he noticed in the window a group of small, dusty paintings that had been there for years. Intrigued by American primitives, Caldor bought them for $2.00 each, and asked for more.

Grandma Moses' daughter-in-law told him she thought the woman had ten others, and Caldor asked to buy them all. Upon searching the house, Grandma Moses could find only nine, and not one to disappoint, she quickly cut one of the larger works in half so she'd have ten to complete the set. She was, after all, elderly and alone, and the money was most welcome.

Caldor knew genius when he saw it, and those ten paintings launched a career that spanned the next twenty years. Grandma Moses had her first art show at age 80, and at 95 was commissioned to do a painting for the White House. At age 100 she illustrated the now classic "Visit from Saint Nicholas," at the request of Random House. A few months later, she died, having changed the world of art.

She once said, "If I didn't start painting I would have raised chickens, and I could still do it now. I would never sit back in a rocking chair waiting for someone to help me!" She kept busy with something in her hand, serving others, and was therefore ready when the call came to change her world.

*Lynn Heitritter, sheltering the abused.* Before 1980, Lynn Heitritter's life as the wife of an airline pilot and mother of two young daughters flowed along quite smoothly. But a late-night phone call from the teenage daughter of a family they knew changed everything.

"My dad just raped my sister, and she's run away," the young girl sobbed. "She might try to call you, and if she does, will you help her?"

Lynn's yes started her on a decade of change, and a whole new life mission. The ministry began by inviting these two pain-ridden young girls into the Heitritter home. "If God had showed me the spreadsheet of costs, how the intensity of the girls' emotional pain would impact my family, I probably would have chickened out," Lynn said. During these days of heartbreak and learning, Lynn told the Lord, "If there's anything I can do to prevent this from happening to one other child, tell me."

The idea came to write a book, a handbook and teaching kit for Christian parents, aimed at protecting children from abuse.[2] Lynn expected this to be the end of her journey, but it proved to be only the beginning. Before long, she was being asked to speak at churches and social service agencies. Each talk put her in contact with more victims of abuse. From these contacts, Lynn and her husband Ron decided to start a ministry for the sexually abused, and thus was born *Becomers*, a one-year recovery program aimed at helping women in need.

Lynn is changing her world, but she didn't start with an organizational chart or an appearance on *Donahue*. She did it with what she had in her hand—a home, a stable family, and a heart that could feel the pain of another. That was enough.

## Finding Your Gift by Focusing on the Giving

All this talk about changing the world has to do with using our gifts, of course. All we have in our hand is what God has given us. So far, we've talked mostly about the skills and possessions He's bestowed. But He energizes these skills with the gifts of His Spirit.

Romans 12 presents some of these gifts: prophesying, serving, teaching, encouraging,

---

[2]Lynn Heitritter and Jeanette Vought, *Helping Victims of Sexual Abuse* (Minneapolis, Minn.: Bethany House Publishers, 1989).

giving, leading, and showing mercy.

Sermons and seminars, quizzes and question-naires abound on finding your place in this list of motivational gifts. But I doubt all this fuss is nec-essary. Instead of focusing on uncovering our gift, which can get to be a bit self-centered, I pro-pose we major instead on asking, "What are the needs I see around me? What ideas or skills or possessions do I have to help meet those needs?"

With this kind of focus, we'll worry less about our capabilities, and more about loving and serv-ing. In the process of giving, our "gift" will emerge.

If your gift is showing mercy, for example, you'll look around you and see nothing but hurt-ing hearts. Your answer to "What can I do?" will prompt you to get on the phone, break out the Hallmark cards, and begin inviting wounded ones to lunch so you can listen and share in their heartache.

If you have the gift of serving instead, you'll see frazzled young mothers, and may decide to start a Mother's Morning Out at your church.

If your gift is teaching, the need you'll see will have to do with growth or spiritual immaturity, and you'll get a neighborhood Bible study un-derway, or offer to teach Sunday school.

I doubt we need to spend much time studying about what our gifts are. Rather, if we begin to serve others we'll see where God blesses us and how He uses us best, and our gifts will be obvious to all.

What do you have in your hand? A wooden spoon? It's enough to transform some part of your world if you let God show you how to use it for Him, and empower you while you do.

## Keeping the Plates in Balance

Like the Ed Sullivan Show juggler, I've spent a lot of time just trying to keep the precious plates of my life spinning around so that none of them crash to the floor.

The principles I've shared in these pages have helped me juggle my life. But this I know: I'll fail unless I keep evaluating myself as a mate, mother, and woman with a mission.

I'll fail unless I learn to stand guard against attitudes like false guilt, covetousness, bitterness, comparing, and competing.

I need to keep on establishing in my heart a spirit of acceptance, endurance, and vision to do what I can for God in my corner of the world.

As these things come into focus, I will no longer need to worry about frantically keeping the plates in balance. I'll be simply devoted to Christ, and from His life balance flows. The plates may need my nudges, but when I'm devoted to Christ, the burden will no longer be mine alone. He will share it, and together we'll keep life simple and full of joy.